■ ■ ■   W9-AFO-174

Bick Publishing House's
AWARD WINNING NONFICTION AND FICTION
For Teens & Young Adults

3 ALA Notable Books • Christopher Award
3 New York Public Library Best Books for Teens
VOYA Honor Book • YALSA Nominated Quick Picks for Teens
3 *ForeWord Magazine* Best Book of the Year Awards
International Book of the Month Selection
Junior Literary Guild Selection
2 Independent Publisher Book Awards

PUBLISHERS WEEKLY calls Carlson's *Girls Are Equal Too: The Teenage Girl's How-to-Survive Book*, "Spirited, chatty, polemical...A practical focus on psychological survival." ALA Notable Book.

SCHOOL LIBRARY JOURNAL says of her book *Talk: Teen Art of Communication*, "Explores philosophical and psychological aspects of communication, encourages young people." *The Teen Brain Book: Who and What Are You*, "Practical and scientifically-based guide to the teen brain." *In and Out of Your Mind: Teen Science*, "Thought-provoking guide into the mysteries of inner and outer space." New York Public Library Best Books for Teens.

THE NEW YORK TIMES BOOK REVIEW says of Carlson's YA Science Fiction novel *The Mountain of Truth*, "Anyone who writes a teenage novel that deals with a search for the Truth must have a great respect for the young...speaks to the secret restlessness in the adolescent thinker." ALA Notable Book.

KIRKUS REVIEWS YA novel *The Human Apes*, "Vastness of this solution to the human dilemma...." ALA Notable Book.

PUBLISHERS WEEKLY says of *Where's Your Head? Psychology for Teenagers*, co-authored by Dale Carlson and Hannah Carlson, M. Ed., C.R.C. "Psychological survival skills...covers theories of human behavior, emotional development, mental illnesses and treatment." Christopher Award.

THE MIDWEST BOOK REVIEW says of *Who Said What: Philosophy for Teens*, "Evocative, thought-provoking compilation and very highly recommended reading for teens and young adults." VOYA Honor Book.

SCHOOL LIBRARY JOURNAL says of *Stop the Pain: Teen Meditations*, "Much good advice is contained in these pages." New York Public Library Best Books for Teens.

■ ■ ■

■ ■ ■

Praise For
UNDERSTAND YOUR SELF

"I would like to congratulate you for the book. The meticulous study of the formation of a self and its suffering, and the exercises given at the end of each chapter make *Understand Your Self* a practical manual for the understanding of oneself."

— Kishore Khairnar, M. Sc., Director, Krishnamurti Education Trust

"Dale Carlson is able to demonstrate the psychological structure of the self using easy to understand language, so that it becomes clear the self is an illusion created by thought and not a reality. Carlson's book demonstrates that human culture and education have perpetuated the idea of the separate self, and how much psychological pain it causes ourselves and each other when the self is not properly understood. Understanding the self, our selves, may be the most important task we have as members of the human race."

— Kenneth Teel, M.S.W. Housing Provider for the Homeless

"*Understand Your Self* is a valuable introduction to the process and necessity of questioning one's thoughts. It intends to help teens transcend negative thought patterns in order to recognize their inner truth.

A manual for self-awareness for those who are struggling with identity, personal, cultural, or otherwise. This book provides tools needed to find purpose in a very modern world."

— Taylor Bratches, 24, Young Adult Editor, Bick Publishing House

"*Understand Your Self* examines the most elusive notion throughout the history of neuroscience: the human self. In a thorough and investigative manner, Carlson explores the illusions we have about the human psyche and the stories we tell ourselves about who and what we are. This manual shows us how to truly understand the structure of ourselves."

— Jason DeFrancesco, Yale New Haven Hospital

■ ■ ■

UNDERSTAND YOUR SELF

UNDERSTAND YOUR SELF

Dale Carlson

Co-author:
Kishore
Khairnar, M.Sc.

Pictures by
Carol Nicklaus

BICK
PUBLISHING
HOUSE

Bick Publishing House   2012   Madison, Connecticut

Edited by Director Editorial Ann Maurer
Science Editors Hannah Carlson, M. Ed., LPC,
   Jason DeFrancesco, Ken Teel
Young Adult Editor Taylor Bratches
Book Design by Jennifer A. Payne, Words by Jen
Cover Design by Greg Sammons

www.bickpubhouse.com

Library of Congress Cataloging-in-Publication Data

Carlson, Dale Bick.
 Understand your self / by Dale Carlson and Kishore Khairnar ; pictures by Carol
Nicklaus.
    p. cm.
 Includes bibliographical references and index.
 ISBN 978-1-884158-36-0 (alk. paper)
 1. Self-perception in adolescence--Juvenile literature. 2. Self--Juvenile litera-
ture. 3. Self-consciousness (Awareness)--Juvenile literature. 4. Adolescent
psychology--Juvenile literature. I. Khairnar, Kishore. II. Nicklaus, Carol. III. Title.
 BF724.3.S35C37 2012
 155.2--dc22
                        2012022796

AVAILABLE THROUGH:
• Distributor: BookMasters, Inc., AtlasBooks Distribution,
   Tel: (800) BookLog, Fax: (419) 281-6883
• Baker & Taylor Books
• Ingram Book Company
• Follett Library Resources, Tel: (800) 435-6170 Fax: (800) 852-5458
• Amazon.com

Or: Bick Publishing House
16 Marion Road
Branford, CT 06405
Tel and Fax: (203) 208-5253

Printed by McNaughton & Gunn, Inc. USA

IN DEDICATION

To all of us everywhere who were hoaxed into believing there is such a thing as a 'self' by previously hoaxed generations: look down your shirt or at any MRI of brain or body, and you will not find anyone at home.

ACKNOWLEDGMENTS

To Kishore Khairnar, Dialogue Director of the Krishnamurti Education Trust, for his greatness of understanding and dedication to teaching.

To Hannah Carlson, Director of Dungarvin's Group Homes for Adults with Mental Disabilities, for the astuteness of her psychological insights.

To Ann Maurer, for her constant editorial guidance.

To Carol Nicklaus, for her award-winning art.

To Greg Sammons, for his awarded covers.

To Jen Payne, for her impeccable taste in interior design.

To Ken Teel, Jason DeFrancesco, and Taylor Bratches for their Young Adult editing and thoughtful attention.

TABLE OF CONTENTS

THE SECRET OF LIFE

When I was a teenager, I was absolutely certain that there was a key to living and understanding life, that I was missing that key, and that other people knew the secret I did not somehow share. When I grew older, I realized most people had no more clues to the secret of living a happy, connected life instead of a lonely, scared life than I did. I wanted the secret of the joy of being alive and I wanted to learn what to do about life's pains. I scrambled through my life blindly.

Listening at Keyholes

But I kept listening at keyholes. I was not interested in hand-me-down platitudes and second-hand knowledge. I was not interested in rules or following someone else's authority. I was interested in learning how to learn the meaning of life for myself. I did this by reading. I found thinkers who understood my question, and they all, from Socrates to Jesus to Buddha to Krishnamurti, from Freud and Daniel Dennett, to Stephen Hawking and Stephen Jay Gould, all of them seemed to say the same thing in different ways. The source of suffering is the frightened self. Since it is the self with its self-centered fears and desires that causes human miseries, understanding that self—self-knowledge—is the key to understanding the problems of human life.

Listening to Oneself

By self-knowledge, I mean learning to know what has made you the way you are, not only physically, but psychologically. This includes understanding that you share an evolutionary, biological, and species history with all human beings, as well as your own family, cultural, and personal heredity. Some of what you have inherited is good to enjoy, the pleasures of food, sex, the sunlight. Some of what you have inherited, through evolution and culture, like violence, conflict, hatred, you can learn to stop acting on. Changing your patterns of thought and behavior through this self-knowledge is the key to freedom from the agonies of fear, loneliness, and insecurity your own conditioning causes you. Life does not have to be so hard to live.

None of the desires or fears you have inherited or been taught have to rule you. Look at everything you feel, think, and how you behave with new eyes. A pain in the self can be a great teacher: the joy of getting beyond it, an even greater one. It even turns out self-knowledge is the basis for relationship and the end of human loneliness.

— Dale Carlson
  Adapted from *The Teen Brain Book:*
  Who and What Are You?

Introduction

WHAT IS A HUMAN BEING?

Young people sit in classrooms and at dinner tables all over the world and wonder why the adults talk about everything but the actual truth about themselves.

The teen brain may not develop fully until the mid-twenties, but it is smart enough to discover that while adult human beings seem to know so much science about technology, about the universe, about how things work, they seem to have practically no understanding of themselves as human beings.

What is a human being?

Why are our lives the way they are, with so much outer cruelty and inner psychological pain?

Why do we feel happy only once in a while, and all the loneliness and pain in between?

Why Don't We Understand Ourselves?

Why don't we understand ourselves better so we can change our own suffering and stop making other people suffer?

Why don't we change? Can we change? Can we change ourselves fundamentally to stop human psychological pain?

How we can learn to understand ourselves and change what doesn't work is the subject of this book *Understand Your Self*.

When you want to look at your face, you use the help of a mirror. But when we want to observe ourselves psychologically, inwardly, is there a mirror we can use? The great philosopher

J. Krishnamurti teaches us that there is such a mirror. The mirror is our relationships: our relationships to each other; to possessions, to money; to escapes like drugs, video games, sex; our relationships to country, religion, family.

Do we understand the differences between love and dependency? Between giving and getting? That including only some people in a group like family or country excludes others, even to the point of war and killing?

Can we understand our need to escape the human psychological pain from fear and loneliness through distraction in entertainment or romance? Can we go even deeper and look at our common evolutionary human past and see that all human beings have the same ancient fears and needs we had back in cave-dwelling days?

We Don't Have to Hurt Ourselves

Most important, can we see that we do not have to go on living like this? That we do not have to hurt ourselves and each other any more if we just pay attention to our thoughts and past behaviors and not act them out again and again?

The trouble is the unbalanced development of the technological and the psychological. Our technological ability to kill and compete has far outstripped our psychological ability to cooperate. This is a major cause of all conflict and suffering in human life. We must learn about ourselves, our reactions of fear and anger and need and loneliness, and then not act them out in order to stop this endless chain of giving and getting pain. Watch what we feel, think, do, and then behave well anyway so we don't pass the pain on. Watch that you don't accumulate more psychological memory. Technical memory is necessary. If you can't remember your language you can't function. If you forget how to do brain surgery, you can't operate. If you forget that fire hurts, you'll burn yourself again. But psychological memories are not necessary, how you got hurt, the guilt of hurting others, family and religious and cultural grudges. Pay attention when these come up, of course, but don't act on them, and you'll break the chain of hurting yourself and others.

You don't need any special time or place to observe yourself in relationship to how you live your life, or your relationship to other people, places, and things. As you go through your day, pay attention to your reactions—and then respond responsibly instead of spreading more hurt around like a nasty virus. What's needed is not to go to some special place: learn about yourself as you live your daily life.

All that's needed is your own interest in understanding yourself.

— Kishore Khairnar, M.Sc.
   Director, Krishnamurti Education Trust

Chapter One
THE SELF

■ ■ ■

"The trouble with brains, it seems, is that when you look in them, you discover that there's nobody home. No part of the brain is the thinker that does the thinking or the feeler that does the feeling."

— Daniel Dennett, *Consciousness Explained*

"We suffer from a hallucination...that "I myself" is a separate center of feeling and action."

—Alan Watts, *The Book: The Taboo Against Knowing Who You Are*

■ ■ ■

What Is a Self?

We all have something we call my self. You will see this if you watch how much time you spend thinking about that self.

How am I feeling?

How am I doing?

How do I look?

Who likes me?

Who doesn't?

Am I going to win or lose out, find a place in life or fall through a black hole somewhere in the universe?

What do I want for lunch?

Haven't you noticed the eternal announcements in your head of 'I want that' or 'I don't want this'? 'I feel good' or "I feel bad'?

And then there are all the people outside your head who keep on asking questions of whoever is inside your head, like 'what are you doing?', 'what have you done?', 'what are you going to do?', 'have you found yourself yet?'

If you have spent any time at all thinking about the self everyone talks about, your self, that is, you may have discovered that it never feels quite real. You are absolutely, entirely correct. There is no physical, neural 'self' anywhere in brain or body. The self is only an idea we human beings have created, and what's more, the idea comes and goes. When you are paying attention to something else, the 'you' of you often fades in and out.

Every Human Brain Creates the Hallucination, the Illusion of a Self

Our brains create the idea of a self out of our own memories, feeling, and thoughts, out of our own stories of our lives. The brain simply calls the hero of our lives—'I', 'myself.'

We have the sensation that a 'me' lives somewhere inside our skins, lonely and separate from everything else, peering out at the world. If you are paying attention to that self, yourself, you will notice that much of the time, the 'you' of you feels anxious, or lonely, or scared. And since you have also experienced pleasure and fun, you know these two sensations will provide escape from the bad feelings. So that 'me' looks for all kinds of pleasures not just for fun, but for escape, from drugs and sex to entertainment and distractions of all kinds. The trouble with

THE SELF IS ONLY
AN IDEA WE HUMAN
BEINGS HAVE
CREATED.

escapes and pleasures is they don't work for very long. And they don't really ever fully satisfy our eternal human neediness. Don't take my word for this. See for yourself. Don't you have to keep repeating the pleasure because it doesn't last?

In its lonely fear, the self not only tries pleasure that doesn't last for long. It creates more pain by fighting to defend itself, and ends by hurting and being hurt.

So because humans have invented a self, we spend our lives afraid of living which is painful to the self, and dying which is the self's end.

The Brain's Best Kept Secret:
There Is No Such Thing as a Self

But this 'me', this 'I', this "self" shows up on no X-ray, no MRI, no PET scan. There is no little person, no small 'you' anywhere physically inside your body or your brain, no actual, single physical thing as a self. There is no little person in your brain where a singular you lives. You have no actual place in your brain (or your heart, for that matter, in case you were looking down inside your shirt for your self). No CAT scan has ever found you.

What Are You?

What *you are* is scattered all over your brain—a collection, a group of thoughts, feelings, ideas, memories stored in the patterns of your brain's synaptic connections between your brain cells—*that's what you are!* And because new thoughts, feelings, experiences, behaviors, and reinterpreted memories occur all the time, your brain reinvents you, the image you have of yourself, that is, all the time. So the 'you' of you is just the

THE TROUBLE WITH BRAINS, IT SEEMS,
IS THAT WHEN YOU LOOK IN THEM, YOU
DISCOVER THERE'S NOBODY HOME.

nerve wirings of your brain, as we discussed in an earlier book *The Teen Brain: Who and What are You?*

All this is why you have a hunch sometimes that there's no real you, that *you* aren't actually *there*. Trust your hunch. *You* aren't *there*. Not as a single entity. You're a collection of changing and changeable nerve connections spread all over your brain.

As neuroscientist Joseph LeDoux says, "People don't come preassembled, but are glued together by life...The particular patterns of synaptic connections in an individual's brain, and the information encoded by these connections, are the keys to who that person is." The brain's information comes from our common human evolutionary inheritance, our genes, and from our individual experience—human history and personal history. And pieces of all these histories are scattered all over our brain, not collected in one place.

Neuroscientifically, it seems to many brain scientists like Dr. Daniel Dennett, that no matter where you look inside you, there's nobody at home, no self in there anywhere. Or, as he says in *Consciousness Explained*, "the trouble with brains, it seems, is that when you look in them, you discover *there's nobody home*. No part of the brain is the thinker that does the thinking or the feeler that does the feeling."

The self, it turns out, is an invention of thought, a story that a person's memories put together. There is not an actual, physical 'self' anywhere inside any skull.

There is no small 'you' in residence. There is no 'ghost in the machine', no 'little policeperson' in there directing your traffic, no 'mini-you' anywhere inside you.

Your brain's magic trick extends from creating a 'you' to preventing your ever being able to see this 'you' directly. It's like trying to see your face with your own eyes.

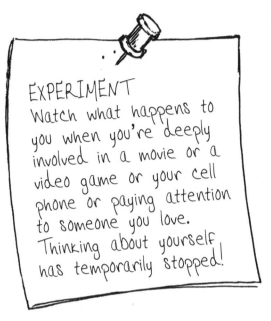

EXPERIMENT: The Vanishing 'I'

You can test for yourself that the 'I' or 'you' of you is not a permanent fixture. Watch what happens to you when you're deeply involved in a movie or a video game or your cell phone or paying attention to someone you love. Thinking about yourself has temporarily stopped. You can tell this because when the involvement stops, you have the feeling 'you' weren't there for a while, and now you have to pull the pieces of yourself together from different parts of your brain. Haven't you had this experience, the feeling of disappearing for a while, then pulling yourself together?

Your Self Is the Ongoing Story
You tell Yourself about Your Life

So, brain scientists tell us there is no central self inside us. Yet, psychologically, our mental processes have invented a self out of our thoughts and feelings, our memories and experiences, our personal and cultural stories, even out of all human evolution. Dr. Sigmund Freud, the 20th century psychoanalyst who studied the effects of the unconscious and subconscious mind, had an equally ingenious student named Carl Jung, who investigated the racial memory shared by the whole human species. Between them, they studied both the personal and evolutionary influences on the formation of a human self. So both species and personal memory have invented the story of ourselves out of the history of our thoughts. And since thoughts about our thoughts change, the story of the 'you' of you not only stretches back millions of years, it goes on changing throughout your life. The 'you' of you, the 'ego', the 'I', whatever you or your favorite psychologist or philosopher likes to call it, evolves. It is never permanent.

The good news is this means that you can change the story of yourself, the 'you' of you. With a new understanding of what a 'you' is, what a 'self' is, *you can change your brain's information and therefore what you are whenever you like.*

**CHANGE YOUR
STORY NOW. BEFORE
AGE SETS IT LIKE
CEMENT.**

If These Are the Facts, Why
Are We Taught So Wrongly

❶ It felt, when we came out of the jungle and began to
consider these matters, as if humans had separate
selves, so that's what people told their children. See
the chapter on the evolution of the self.

❷ Children are also told their survival depends on
thinking and doing what adults tell them.

❸ There was no neuroscientific technology in the jungle
to prove we were wrong about having selves.

Teach Yourself about Yourself

You don't have to understand neuroscience to understand how
what we call the 'self' works.

You just have to look at, to watch, to observe your
relationships to everything in your life. Watch your reactions to
people, to money, to school, to work, to nature, to the universe,
to anything that crosses your path in your everyday life. You
can feel your psychological reactions (who and what you are
attached to for security, who and what you resent or fear) rise
in you at every turn. These reactions make you feel as if there
really is a 'self' who is reacting. But it's just the nerve circuits in
your brain receiving and sending information to the rest of your
body's nervous, muscular, glandular, skeletal systems. It is hard
to remember this is just a physical, material process when it *feels*
personal. Don't let anyone tell you it is easy to remember the

self isn't real and that you can just stop defending it, protecting it, advancing its position in the world all the time.

Because even if there's no self as a physical reality, your brain has invented the feeling, the idea of a self. And that idea, that feeling of self is what causes the pain, the state of emotional, psychological loneliness. There may be times when your self feels confident, happy, free, especially when you get good grades, or the person you fall in love with falls in love with you, too. But even when good moments happen, aren't you also afraid they won't last? Mostly, the idea of a 'self' is a real headache.

Don't let anyone tell you it is easy to dismiss this business of the self. Real or not, the self plagues us like a cloud of gnats.

But by altering attitudes, thinking, and behavior you can change the neuronal circuits all over your brain that house your life's information and so the story of your self. Change your information, and you change your brain and its story, the ongoing story you tell yourself about your life.

And since the self is just a story our thoughts, our brains tell us all the time, waking or sleeping, the self changes with the story you tell yourself about the events in your life, and you can change your own story any time you like. This is especially true in the teen years, because the brain, especially the frontal lobes, doesn't finish developmental maturation until sometime in the twenties.

Change your story now. Before age sets it like cement.

**FEAR AND ANGER
ARE REALLY JUST GHOSTS.**

How Do You Stop the Pain?

What can you do about it when your brain hurts you with fear, anger, loneliness, when you're hurting from rage or panic, shame, guilt, neediness, addiction?

Sometimes we all need the psychological help of professionals. But you can't drag an advisor around with you forever. Sooner or later you have to understand what it is to be a human being, to have a human brain that invents and compares selves.

It is in seeing through your own self and understanding how that self works its tricks so that you can end the self, stop the pain and confusion, and get to the fun and joy of being alive.

The Self May Keep on Coming Back

We know that there have been great minds who finished with the self for once and for all: Jesus, Buddha, Lao Tzu, Lord Rama, Kwan Yin, Krishnamurti. For most of us, while we may end some of our worst forms of selfish self-centeredness, the self keeps coming back. So do know you are not alone if the feeling of having a self with its problems of self-centeredness—fear, anger, the feelings of not fitting in or being good enough—all these feelings may come back over and over again, as well as the problem behaviors that go with the feelings. But once you begin to understand that these feelings of fear and anger are really just ghosts, you can deal with them as they come up, and end them without acting on them every time something disturbs you.

What helps is to remember not to take our selves, or anyone else's self, personally. The idea of a self is just an evolutionary survival trick to keep the body alive. You are not separate from or much different from anything or anyone else in the universe. It's all just particles.

This book is about understanding how *your* self and therefore how all human selves work. Because give or take the monkey trick of having a talent for music, sports, or juggling plates, all of which are just a bit of atypical neuronal wiring, give or take some damage either through nature or nurture, all members of the human species are as alike as all members of the pussycat species, who, as we know, unlike dogs, all belong to the same family.

How to Go about
Understanding Yourself

■ ■

"I" exist only in relationship to people, things, and ideas,
and in studying my relationship to outward things and
people, as well as to inward things,
I begin to understand myself.

— J. Krishnamurti, *Freedom from the Known*

■ ■

So, if you cannot see yourself as you read this any more than you can see your face without a mirror, how can you see yourself? Relationship is the mirror.

Look in the mirror of your relationships. In the mirror of your relationship to other people, to school, to work, to money, to danger, to your escapes from life into drugs or sex or video games—you can see what you are: full of fear, anxiety, anger, affection, possessiveness, joy.

You don't need psychiatrists, clever books, so-called adults with authority, to tell you about yourself.

You can read the book of yourself on your own.

Chapter Two

THE HUMAN BRAIN'S BIG MISTAKE, THE ISOLATION OF SELVES

■ ■ ■

"The sense of self is perfectly natural. All forms of life must have some boundaries. Even the one-celled organism has a membrane that outlines its being. Our complex self-identification may be an evolved outgrowth of that single cell's outer membrane."

—Wes Niskar, philosopher, *Buddha's Nature: Evolution as a Practical Guide to Enlightenment*

■ ■ ■

Human Loneliness, The Beginning

In the beginning was our mistake, the human brain's error in thinking. Humans live as if we were 'in here' and the rest of the world is 'out there.' Niskar says, "We experience our human life and society as different from nature, somehow detached from universal laws and the unfolding of biological evolution."

Evolutionary and genetic scientists from Charles Darwin to Richard Dawkins have proved that all life evolved from the same single-celled creatures, just as cosmologists and physicists like Albert Einstein and Stephen Hawking have shown us that the whole universe and everything in it evolved out of a single hot ball of matter.

But human brains experience human lives as different from nature, separate from the rest of the universe, even lost somehow among the stars.

This mistake in our thinking, that we are outside of and separate from nature and the unfolding of the universe, creates a fearful loneliness, and therefore our inner conflicts and outer conflicts. Developing this wrong idea that we are separate beings instead of part of the universal flow is killing us. Psychologically, the terror of loneliness creates mental illness, addictions of all kinds. And physically, the false idea of having only a self to depend on makes us greedy for security, for more of everything, and so we kill each other and destroy nature to grab the most resources. And we all end up, not more, but less secure than ever. We must correct for our evolutionary brain's mistake, and understand we are not alone but interconnected and interdependent on one another's welfare.

Why did we do it, make the mistake of seeing ourselves as separate? How did we learn this maladaptive trick? Remember: not all of evolution's mutations work out well! We may have to lend evolution a hand to save ourselves. With insight into her tricky accidents, we can understand and therefore change the course of evolution itself.

THE IDEA
THAT WE ARE
SEPARATE
BEINGS INSTEAD
OF PART OF THE
UNIVERSAL FLOW
IS KILLING US.

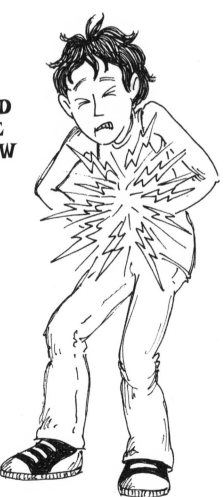

Evolution of Life
Biology's major rules of life are:

❶ Stay alive yourself. Eat, breathe, get a move on when necessary.

❷ Reproduce, so when you die, the species stays alive.

To remain alive yourself, you have to tell the difference between what you can eat and what will eat you.

To keep your species alive, you have to distinguish who or what is an appropriate mate and who or what is not.

Evolution's Gift to Us Is a Two-Way Sword
Evolution's great gift to the human species was not strength or speed, flight or size. It was intellect, a large brain and its increasingly complicated neural wiring with an ability to make distinctions and divisions and find differences better than any other species.

Unfortunately, human brains made the mistake of confusing the significance of '*different*.' We have misinterpreted 'differences' as 'threats.' If you are not exactly like me in size, shape, color, thoughts, beliefs, behaviors, you are a threat. Gender difference can be pleasurably exciting. Most other differences scare us. Our human ability to distinguish 'difference' so we don't get killed by predators, has turned everything and everyone external to the protective envelope of our own skin into a threat. This is, of course, the origin of prejudice, racism, nationalism, religious crusades, school cliques, and street gangs at war.

WE HAVE MISINTERPRETED 'DIFFERENCES' AS 'THREATS.'

As Niskar says, "The dividing intellect that gave us power over things also severed the primal umbilical cord; it cut us off from the rest of creation." This even includes dividing ourselves from each other until it feels as if each of us is entirely alone living inside our own box, the envelope of our own skin.

The very nature of the self is to isolate itself for protection, build walls, differentiate in its own self-importance the importance of others, and therefore suffer loneliness and suspicion. The lonely suffering of this isolation creates another problem as well: it makes us seek relief from our suffering through pleasure, the pleasures of sex, money, power, position, drugs, entertainment, the possession of another human being.

Unlike other species (as far as we know), the human brain developed conscious thought. Thought has turned these merely physical divisions into a psychological division between SELF and NOT-SELF. This division between ourselves and the rest of nature produced not only loneliness, but the exploitation of everything and everyone not the SELF.

We may have danced for joy when we invented our almighty SELF. We were important, superior in our own eyes and in the eyes of our gods. But we had just signed our own death warrants as a species. Our psychological separation from earth and sky, from other creatures, our feeling of dominion and entitled superiority, has turned us into greedy children, taking and smashing whatever we want until the nursery is a wreck and there is nothing left.

The Dividing of People into Separate Selves Will Kill Us

This looking out for just the 'self' will kill us if we fail to see that in fact, we are not isolated and that everything affects everything else. The feeling of 'alone' is not in fact an actual fact. Physics has taught us that everything in the universe, as we have said, is made of minute particles, what appears solid is not solid at all, and therefore *boundaries are porous.* This makes everything and everyone interactive and therefore interconnected.

You may well, at this point, wonder why, either at school or at home, this is not discussed with you over and over again. Is it because your parents and teachers were never told by their parents and teachers? Can you bring up this question, this major problem of human existence yourself, in class or at the dinner table? No matter what the reaction, let no one tell you that understanding the psychological structure of your own and therefore all selves is not the most important of matters.

Any physicist will tell you—everything in the universe affects everything else. Scientists will also tell you that while all living forms have an outer membrane, a skin, a container, a boundary, *these outer shells are not solid.* Everything exchanges particles all the time. And not just on Earth—microscopic neutrinos from outer space bombard and penetrate your human skin and everything else on Earth all the time.

Ultimately, it is connection not difference that matters.

ULTIMATELY, IT IS CONNECTION NOT DIFFERENCE THAT MATTERS.

Are We Just Blind or Just Scared?

Is it blind arrogance, ignorance, or terror that makes humans put the human brain at the pinnacle of creation, instead of understanding, as Stephen Jay Gould says in his book *Full House*, we are only a twig on the bush of life, not the star on top of the tree? Intellect with its divisions and facets is only one possibly faulty survival tool—and has nothing necessarily to do with intelligence, understanding the truth.

Human thought has produced both language and culture. With the verbal education of its young, it passes on not only practical survival information but its mistaken ideas as well. Along with the instructions on how to use a car and a computer, we pass on ideas, especially the idea of the false division of

EXPERIMENT

What labels have you been given to separate you out from others?

Can you peel them off and join the whole human race?

us from nature, the universe, each other, from generation to generation. We do this often in the name of politics, nationalism, religion, family pride.

EXPERIMENT: Name Your Labels, Peel Them Off

Examine some of these questions and statements.

"Who is mommy's and daddy's special, unique child? Remember that you're better or at least different from those other children!"

"Remember: you are a boy, an American, an Indian Brahmin, Muslim, Chinese, Polish, black, white, yellow, brown, Jewish, Christian, Native American, Latino, that you belong to this family, not those across the street, you are a girl, LGTB, poor and street, middle class and respectable…."

What other labels, categories, differentiations, countries, religions, cliques, groups, genders (remember there or 4-6 genders listed now) have been laid on you?

Has anybody ever said to you, "You'll never be lonely because you are part of a whole gorgeous Earth with nearly 7 billion people to keep you company, that revolves around a star that's part of a galaxy with a hundred or more billion stars in a universe of countless galaxies among possibly even more universes?—and that makes you responsible to and for everything and everything responsible to and for you?"

Have you been told something the *Talmud* says: "We do not see things as they are, but as we are."

Have you been reminded that what Jesus meant in the Sermon on the Mount by "The meek shall inherit the earth," were those without self-centeredness?

Interesting, isn't it!

WE DIVIDE OURSELVES FROM EACH OTHER UNTIL IT FEELS AS IF EACH OF US IS ENTIRELY ALONE.

The Human Brain's Main Capacities

1 Its ancient, evolutionary automatic functions, like breathing, keep us alive.

2 It takes in information from the five senses, processes it, stores it in memory circuits as thought and feeling.

3 It is capable of attention and understanding.

Science, by understanding and paying attention to facts—not conditioned, cultural, divisive hopes, dreams, and old stories— is showing us our oneness with all things in the universe.

Our own fresh and new daily attention (not old thought) to our lives and relationships, to everything we are doing and thinking and feeling, can do the same as science—uncover the daily truth about the ongoing river of living for ourselves. Instead of listening to old myths and misconceptions, learn for yourself what's going on.

■ ■

"Human beings have reached what may well be a pivotal stage in their evolution. They have been created by the universe, in the universe, as an integral part of the universe. They have passed through a difficult period when their strong day-to-day experience of selfhood and their cultural conditioning have made them feel detached from the reality in which they are permanently embedded. And now they are beginning to see beyond the self again into the truth of their condition."

—David Darling, *Zen Physics*

■ ■

Thought and Insight: Intellect and Intelligence

Thought is the collection in your brain's circuits of all your accumulated information. This is your intellect.

Insight is new, moment-by-moment discovery of whether that information is correct or not. This is intelligence, to have fresh insight all the time into old information, as well as new. Most people live their days on old information.

The Brain Is a Recorder

The brain records, but not always accurately, what it experiences. It also edits and changes those experiences as you go on living your life, so your memories change, not always accurately.

Your brain records your parents' and teachers' words from back forever. Your brain records nice or awful things your friends said to you yesterday. Your brain records the smells of foods and flowers, information from the Internet, the words of popular songs, what is cool to wear or say.

Your brain records, all human brains record, information collected for millions of years about what is good to eat, what is poison, how to hide for safety, all the particular group and cultural information collected by your family and you personally.

Along with language, what to eat, and how to dress in your particular climate and civilization, what work is appropriate for your class, caste, sex, and position in life, you are also taught either by words or behavior to think the way your parents and friends think. That includes:

- What you are supposed to want

- What you are supposed to do with your life

- Who you are supposed to like, hate, be for or against

- What is and isn't important—money, or success, or God, or popularity

You know the outcome. Your personality gets formed out of all this. And all this makes you feel as if there's a someone inside you. We're all afraid of living and afraid of dying. So we go along with the help our brains get in inventing a self for a sense of security. Of course, we're not stupid, so we also spend our lives suspecting it's all a hoax and our selves aren't really real at all. We're right, of course. The self is a meme (just a cultural idea that is passed on), not a gene (a gene is a physical fact).

But habit, fear of a great void, and the need for a sense of security, insist on there being an idea of someone in charge of all those firing neurons in the brain. That someone in charge, we are told, is called ME, I, MYSELF.

How do you look at this, at the behavior of the human brain for yourself? If you bring your attention to the activities of your self—your thoughts, your feelings, your actions—you can see this thing at work.

Chapter Three

RELATIONSHIPS ARE YOUR MIRROR

■ ■ ■

"All life is a movement in relationship.
There is no living thing on earth which is
not related to something or other."

—Krishnamurti, *Relationships: to Oneself,
to Others, to the World*

"A human being...experiences himself, his
thoughts and feelings as something separated from the
rest...a kind of optical illusion of his consciousness.
This delusion is a kind of prison for us...our task
must be to free ourselves from this prison."

—Albert Einstein, *The Expanded Quotable Einstein*

■ ■ ■

Why Understand Yourself?

It is as important to have a good relationship with yourself as
with others, because you can't treat anyone any better than you
treat yourself.

If you are critical and mean to you, you'll be critical and
mean to others.

And you cannot understand other people if you do not understand yourself, your own personality. All our personalities are, anyway, are how we handle whatever people or situations come our way. The self, your self, anybody's self or personality, is put together by knee-jerk reactions to a particular set of genes, a particular culture, and a particular education. Intelligence suggests you look at your own genes, culture, education, your own personal self, and then decide on your own, not according to the authority handed down to you, whether what you have inherited, or how you have been indoctrinated, is right for you. Selves, personalities, can be horribly distorted by their cultures, like being programmed to die while killing others.

But even without gross distortions, genes and cultures and educational systems seem to run on robotically without reexamination and readjustment. You and future generations are handed down ancient solutions to the problems of living that may never have worked out well in the first place. Answers to the questions young people ask about how to live their lives need constant reexamination and ongoing discussion.

Confusion and Understanding
You are in psychological confusion most of the time, aren't you? Isn't your brain always asking you questions like:

- What do I do about my relationships with this or that friend?

- What is the point of going to school?

- What am I going to do with my life? Is there any meaning to my life? Why is life so hard?

- What is life?

- What is education for, to live the same grinding life my parents live, always worried and stressed out?

- Do I try to get along with society, do what my parents, teachers, and everybody else seem to expect of me?

- Or do I rebel against falling off the cliff with the rest of the sheep and go my own way alone?

- If I go it alone, won't I be lonely or attacked or left to starve?

- What is death, and why do I sometimes think that death would at least end all this struggling with my life and how to live it. Why is life so hard I spend most of my life trying to escape it, with TV, the Internet, games, movies, sex, drugs, alcohol, gossip, sports.

- Why are some people starving, and some have yachts and six houses?

- Is war right or wrong? Is it ever right to kill another human being, and if it is the wrong solution, how do we protect ourselves, our families, tribes, countries, gangs?

- Where is security, in career, marriage, money? What's wrong with me that I can't seem to find the answers to any of these questions?

- Who or what am I anyway and how do I find out?

- What is love?

- Why bother with these questions? Why not just get on with my life instead of asking questions?

Because the human brain questions everything automatically. It has an evolutionary survival drive to discover the nature of everything, to be curious, to question, to explore its environment, whether outer space or inner space. And then, to reach beyond its grasp. Which can become something of a problem if you don't know what you are doing or why you are doing it.

So you might as well begin understanding life, your life. Insight into these questions begins with understanding yourself, your behavior and the reactions which make up your personality, not once and for all, but in every moment, in every relationship in your life.

We Can, We Must, Change
Our Own Evolutionary Path

Evolution, through natural selection of the qualities that seem to work for each species, makes a lot of mistakes, the side effects of mutation. The way our so-called superior brains work in our human species has a major flaw we must correct

NOTHING PHYSICAL
IN THE UNIVERSE
IS SOLID. ALL THINGS
ARE POROUS AND
EXCHANGE PARTICLES.

by understanding our selves and how we work. Because living forms have membranes, skins to hold in their insides, 'me' and 'not me' have been mistaken for the separation of one person from everything and everybody else. And it's an error that's as catching as the flu we pass on from one person to another—worst of all to our young. We think to strengthen them by reinforcing a sense of self—when all we do is reinforce their sense of apartness.

As we have discovered already, physics, biology, and other forms of science show us that skins, membranes, edges *are not solid—nothing physical in the universe is solid. All things are porous and exchange particles.* This is as true for human tissue as everything else. What is inside you, physically and psychologically, what is inside your body and contained in the equally material thought, mood, and emotional circuits of your brain—all of it leaks out into and affects the atmosphere and people around you.

What You Are Is Transmitted
to All Human Consciousness

So just as a tree breathes out its oxygen and you breathe it in, and you breathe out carbon dioxide and the tree takes it in, all life affects all life. The very breath you breathe out, others breathe in. If your breath is bad from anger, that's what you pass on. But the same goes for affection and good will!

Yourself affects everybody and everything else, including your own body. Learn to understand it and its behavior now and every moment of your life from now on so you go through life not hurting yourself or anyone else. Look around you. See all the violence and suffering, not just in the larger world of war and starvation, but the pain in your own home, in school, in your own family, in your friends, inside you.

How to Understand Yourself
through Your Relationships

The constantly changing thought and emotional circuits of the living brain that create the illusion of self cannot be put under a microscope. This is because nobody alive has yet been willing to donate their living brain to science. We don't even know if we have the science or insight to understand what we might discover.

So, since we can't examine this self we've created physically in the brain, how do we understand, how can we see our selves?

We can see ourselves, therefore, only through our relationships. All life is in relationship, to people, to nature, to the things we own or want, to the ideas we are taught by our countries, cultures, religions.

We can see ourselves every moment of the day in how we relate to everything both outside and inside us. You can watch how you react to a person outside you who does or does not say hello. You can watch your thoughts of a person, angry or loving or fearful, who comes into your head.

Don't Be A Brain-Jerk

But watch your thoughts without doing anything about them for a while. Watch your reactions without acting on them right away. Leave a gap between your reactive thoughts and your behavior! Whatever you feel or think will subside with the next thought or feeling or distraction if you just wait long enough. With practice, you can actually observe this process for yourself.

And then your behavior will be what you want it to be, and not just a chemistry-jerk reaction to whatever has been stuffed into your brain by someone else.

Relationship Acts Like a Mirror of Yourself

Take a look at anyone you know or someone you don't know, think of anything from money to sex to school to work to parents: how do you feel? What do you feel? What thoughts go through your mind? Do you feel loving or angry or sad or lonely or scared or guilty or anxious about the different people in your life? What are you thinking or feeling when you consider the subject of money? Sex? Work? And what do you do about your feelings and thoughts? Do you act on them? Stuff them back inside you? Try to escape them?

When you feel guilty, anxious, stupid, ugly, where do those feelings come from? Who said to feel these ways? Why is your brain always talking to itself? All this yelling at yourself is why we run away from being alone. The alternative to escape is to stand still and understand these voices. You'll find out that insight, understanding, will dissolve them. *This is what meditation is: to pay attention to life and what's going on inside you*

as well as outside and understand, not run away into some pleasure.
Pleasure is natural—always enjoy what is going on. Just don't
use it addictively as an escape from understanding yourself.
The trick in self-awareness is to pay attention to the self in
your brain all the time. We all go to sleep on ourselves sometimes,
escape sometimes, but as much as possible stay awake to what's
going on inside you in reaction to what's going on outside you,
especially when you are hurt or afraid.

Change

Because you can change the *you* of you with every response,
every moment, or else build up habits of reaction until you
end up living your life like a robot. Remember, a lot of your
automatic reactions go back millions, even billions, of years. A
lot of your reactions are just cultural and personal conditioning,
like animals trained for the circus so their performances and
characters can be controlled. All these trained reactions are
your 'me.'

Change your automatic responses by observing them and
making more appropriate responses. *Appropriate response is the
root of responsibility.*

From now on, look at everything inside you and outside
you with 'new eyes' not old reactions. New eyes allow you to
respond rightly to whatever happens. Old reactions just repeat
the past over and over again with all its mistakes and hurts.
New eyes will bring new behavior, intelligent behavior. And
new behavior will rewire the circuits in your brain and bring
change not only in your brain but everyone else's, since all
human consciousness is as connected in behavior as the stars
in our galaxy.

SO, WHAT DO YOU LOOK

LIKE IN RELATIONSHIP?

EXPERIMENT: The Mirror of Relationship

An experiment will give you the beginning of a psychological portrait of yourself.

Go somewhere to be alone, your room, the back yard, an empty car. Bring pad and pencil. For some reason, our brains edit less when we write than when we just think about something.

At the top of a page, write down the name of someone, your mother, for instance, or a friend. Under that name, write down a list of what makes you uncomfortable or happy about that person. Now turn the page over and write down a matching list of what you do and feel about each feeling of pain or pleasure. Do you run? Get angry? Try to please? Crave more? Cry?

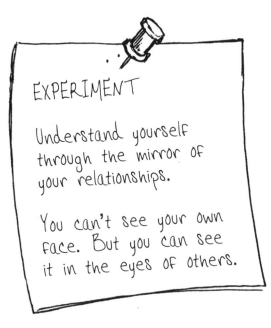

EXPERIMENT

Understand yourself through the mirror of your relationships.

You can't see your own face. But you can see it in the eyes of others.

You will begin to see a psychological picture of yourself in relationship. What makes you feel angry, sad, frightened, happy, or safe appears on one side of the page. What you do about those thoughts and feelings appears on the other side. The first page tells you about your reactions, your thoughts and feelings. The second page tells you about your response and behavior. This experiment will give you a portrait of yourself in relationship to the other people in your life. The more people you do this kind of inventory on, the more you'll learn about your habitual reactions to when you feel fear or anger, judgmental, threatened, joy or pleasure. Once you spot your habitual reactions to your feelings, they no longer have to drag you like wild horses down blind alleys. Do inventories at least on your primal relationships: mother, father, brother, sister. Do a best friend, a teacher, a boss. Some feelings may appear over and over, like the fear of abandonment, like anger in the face of criticism which is based in that fear.

In later chapters, we'll do the same experiment with your reactions in relationship to education, money, sex, marriage, religion, God, and all the other people, places, institutions, possessions, and things that come up in human life.

Life happens. It's what you do about what happens that tells you about your self and what you are. You don't need experts to understand yourself. You can listen to your own brain talking to you! *We not only can think, we can listen to ourselves thinking!* And writing down what you hear makes you listen better, rationalize and edit yourself less.

Here is what I mean. Begin with what you don't like about the people in your life, *and what you do about it, how you behave.* This is more telling than what you do like.

MOTHER

What I Don't Like	What I Do About It
1. Likes my sister better than me	1. I compete, work hard, get mad at my sister
2. Lectures, yells, humiliates me	2. Shut mother out, talk back, rebel, leave home young, look for someone to rescue me, learn to blame others for my bad feelings, fear, shame
3. Always angry	3. I was always angry back, became an addict to escape bad feelings

What I Do Like	What I Do About It
1. She's fun, entertaining	1. I learn to be fun, entertain
2. She's elegant, arrogant	2. Me, too

It's the second list that tells you about yourself and how you react to people, your usual, knee-jerk reactions to others.

In this silent dialogue with ourselves, remember we are not condemning, judging, justifying ourselves, just looking at how humans feel, think, react, behave. There's no feeling you have, no reaction you have we don't all share. We all have the same human brain, remember. But most people never look at themselves, never take responsibility for their thoughts, feelings, or behaviors. They blame others and act like victims.

The point of this kind of inventory of yourself is that *just because you behaved like this as a child, even as a young teenager, you don't have to spend the rest of your life hanging on to bad feelings and harmful behavior toward yourself and other people.*

Change What Makes You Feel Bad about You: Quick Course

You'll see, in your watchful awareness of yourself in everyday relationships, how you used to and might still react—and stop reaction, by leaving a space, a gap, between your knee-jerk old reactions and your present response.

In other words, by understanding and watching old habits, you can change the self, your self, and change your brain's wiring with bad feelings and painful thoughts.

1 Notice your reactions to everyone and everything. But don't judge them as right or wrong, good or bad.

2 Remember we want security, all living beings want to be safe, and we are taught that if we have certain values, obey certain rules, have certain friends, clothes, stuff,

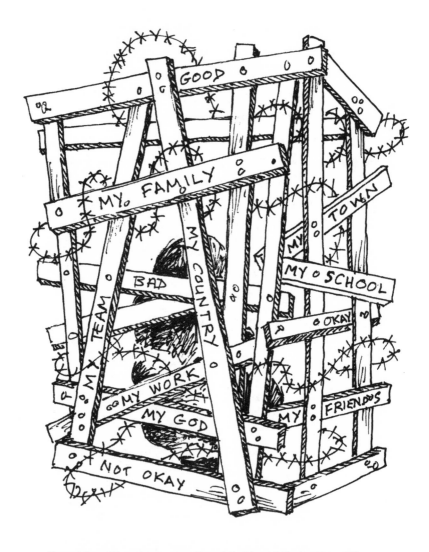

IMAGES AND BELIEF SYSTEMS ARE
PRISONS, NOT FREEDOMS.

belong to a certain, country, tribe, family, religion, go to the right schools, have the right job or profession, we will be safe. (There is no such thing as safety—except learning to live perfectly well without it.)

❸ Remember that all these images and belief systems (do this, you'll get that) are prisons, not freedoms.

❹ If your behavior causes pain to you or anyone else, you can change it. You may find you will have to change it many times, every time it comes up, and that some reactions may continue for a lifetime. Just watch for and stop them when they come up, drop the feelings when they come up—every time they come up. Recovering addicts and alcoholics understand this: We may go on wanting a drink, drug, a shopping spree, more sex, whatever. We just don't act on it, and in a few moments, the craving passes.

❺ Changing your behavior to people changes and rewires the neuronal circuits, the nerve circuits in your brain.

❻ Change your brain and you can change your psychological pain into understanding your own self and everyone else's.

Learning that the self is a myth that we are conditioned to believe in even if it isn't real is the beginning. Drop the myth of the self—and there isn't anything to hurt!

Do this every time the self in you returns. And it will return, for sure.

Chapter Four

SELF AND LOVE, SEX, MARRIAGE, AND RELATIONSHIPS

■ ■ ■

"The demand to be safe in relationship inevitably breeds sorrow and fear. This seeking for security is inviting insecurity. Have you ever found security in any of your relationships?…We are not loved because we don't know how to love…Adoring someone, sleeping with someone, the emotional exchange, the companionship—is that what we mean by love?…If I say 'I love you,' does that exclude the love of the other?"

—J. Krishnamurti, *Freedom from the Known*

"If we weren't so needy, so full of illusions about a magic rescue, so hooked on trying to own someone—in other words, if the conscious goal of romance were stretching our understanding of ourselves and others… romance could be a deep, intimate, sensual, empathetic way of learning through someone else's eyes, feeling with their nerve endings, absorbing another culture or way of life from the inside."

—Gloria Steinem, *Revolution from Within, Romance versus Love*

■ ■ ■

What Is Love?

We look for security in other people, don't we?

We look to our relationships with other people, friends, lovers, family, to provide us with a sense of belonging, to protect us from the fear of isolation and loneliness, to keep us safe from not only physical danger, but from the psychological terror of the great dark emptiness of the unknown universe. We need to matter, to know that it matters that we lived at all.

It's scary out there.

So we huddle. Like sheep.

It is perfectly true that humans have physical needs on which life depends. Like all animals, we need food and water, we need air to breathe. We need clothes since we have no fur or feathers, and shelter from the elements. We need community, from hospitals to the post office. We need the reassuring sight and touch of our own kind for physical and psychological health.

But there is a big difference between the physical dependencies of nature, our evolutionary survival skills, and the needy psychological dependencies human beings form. What we call love.

- Dating and mating love. *(You take care of my needs, I'll do yours.)*

- Family love and parent-child love. *(I'll feed you, you make me look good.)*

- Love of country, religion, God. *(You take care of me, I'll sacrifice to you.)*

What we call love is simply a demand for return on our investment. It is based on the illusion that there is such a thing as safety, security for the illusory self.

Love Is not the Trade-Off of Dependency

Love is freely given. Simply put, love is living with compassionate kindness, meaning love for all, people, animals, the earth, the work you do, not just who'll pay you back or what will bring you money or sex or fame or a temporary feeling of belonging or security. If you do what you do to serve your self, is it love? Can you love another freely without controlling them or depending on them? Can you love your work, your studies or a job, without ambition for yourself?

Loving freely is not a just a question of being a good person (another ambition, actually). Have you noticed how everything and everyone in life changes, moves on, like the clouds in the sky? You'll just get hurt feelings if you try to hang on to anyone or anything. It turns out that the only way not to suffer is not to let the self in you attach like a barnacle to people, places, things, ideologies. Love doesn't hurt. Only dependency hurts. Lean, and off-balance, you'll fall down.

Get Over Yourself

Have you ever heard the expression 'get over yourself'? This is not a matter of being good or virtuous. It's just that the self gets hurt so easily, it's better to get over the idea of self being real altogether.

After all, this thing we call a self only feels real out of habit, neuronal reinforcement. If parents and teachers tell a child often

LOVE IS
FREELY
GIVEN.

enough, the idea that it has a self will become embedded in the brain's nerve cells. If a child is told it is good and satisfactory, it feels all puffed up with the importance of its little self. If a child is ignored or told it is bad, it learns to feel bad, needy, empty, as if its little self is no good. It doesn't even take parents and teachers. The whole world is forever reflecting your behavior like a mirror and calling what is simply behavior a 'self.'

Getting over the idea of actually having a self requires a sense of humor and just paying attention to the way your thought/memory/self works. It also requires curiosity, and the passion to understand your life.

Look at your life with new eyes, not just according to what someone else has told you, or old, conditioned evolutionary thought patterns. And look with affection for your person, for your mental condition, for your emotions. Human affection for yourself as well as other people can override conditioned thoughts and evolutionary reactions.

"Getting over yourself is like getting over a cold in the head. It is just a thought infection, not a normal condition," says philosopher Ray Fisher.

Nature Has Helped Us:
It Is Our Turn to Help Nature

All relationships, whether simple friendship, or the intimate, sexual relationships of romance and marriage, can only be as successful as your ability to understand yourself, your motives, your ways of interacting with people, places, things, and the institutions of your particular culture or society.

You'll discover that most of your ways of relating to anything or anyone are the same as your ways of relating to everyone and everything. To know how you relate is the first step in knowing what and how to change whatever needs changing.

"Nature helped us to evolve physically. We must cooperate with nature to evolve psychologically by mutating, transforming our mind," says physicist and philosopher Kishore Khairnar.

Six hundred years before Jesus, and about two and a half thousand years ahead of Freud, Buddha spoke of Four Truths he had discovered after years of intelligent attention to the state of the human psyche.

❶ All humans suffer.

❷ The bad news is, we cause this psychological pain ourselves through constant wanting.

❸ The good news is we can stop the pain by paying attention to the human evolutionary alarms about survival and safety that go off in us—and behave, not like a human animal, but a humane being.

❹ Here's how. Every action is followed by a consequence, so be careful what you do, think, say, listen to, how you make a living. Make sure you do no harm to yourself or others.

So, we're back to: everything affects everything else on earth and in the universe—everything matters. If you act as if you are separate, not only will the loneliness kill you, the constant greediness of loneliness will kill others.

EXPERIMENT: Thought Prevents Relationship

If at any time this experiment embarrasses or upsets you, stop thinking. Stop thought right in its tracks. Practical thought is necessary. You have to speak a language, drive a car, remember your address. It is psychological thought that causes you pain. Psychological thought is what invents the 'I' and the 'me', and when you stop thought, there's no 'you' to have the thoughts or thought's psychological feelings. You do not want to ignore your thoughts and feelings: you do want to think them through, discuss them with someone, decide what action to take. But most of us tend to repeat our psychological thoughts over and over, and chew over mental distresses as a cow chews and chews her cud. This is just crazy-making and there are ways to stop psychological thought from repeating itself.

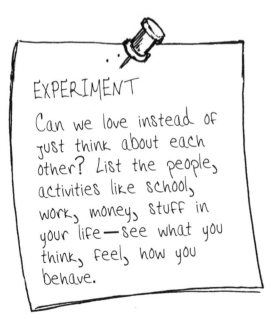

EXPERIMENT

Can we love instead of just think about each other? List the people, activities like school, work, money, stuff in your life — see what you think, feel, how you behave.

Many people use the following suggestions and call them various forms of meditation.

❶ Attention: pay attention to thinking itself, not just what you are thinking.

❷ Distraction: Read a book, play a game. Shift attention to someone else, not your self.

❸ Or go for a walk and turn your eyes into windows instead of mirrors, and look out, not in.

❹ Physical exercise, giving complete attention to the body, and bringing your attention back to the body every time you notice it sneaking back into your thoughts.

The above mental tools are suggested because if you are not embarrassed by yourself as you do the following experiment, you are not doing it correctly. Remember, all human feelings and thoughts are felt and thought by all humans. You are not alone.

The List
Write down the names of:

❶ A best friend
❷ One boyfriend/girlfriend/lover
❸ Mother
❹ Father
❺ Teacher, boss, authority figure

Next to each name, write down the answers to the following questions.

❶ What do you want and need from them?
❷ What qualities do you want them to have?
❸ How do you want them to think of you?

My teenage friend Dana showed me her list.

❶ Best friend: likes me best, is always there for me, thinks I'm right

❷ Boyfriend: loves me only, is always there for me, supports me no matter what

❸ Mother: Want to be her favorite child

❹ Father: Want him to be proudest of me

❺ Teacher, boss, authority figure: Want them to think I'm the smartest kid in the class, on the job, anywhere, and to give me special attention and privileges because of this

Bill Wilson, who founded and wrote the *Twelve Steps and Twelve Traditions of Alcoholics Anonymous,* wrote "Either we tried to play God and dominate those about us, or we had insisted on being over-dependent upon them."

Dana could see quickly that all her relationships were based on her self and others' reactions to that self. None were based on just loving, although just loving did happen when the above conditions were met.

Otherwise, there was hurt. Painful thoughts, painful feelings, all the result of her own dependency and need to control her emotional environment and what people thought and felt about her so she could feel secure. Most of us are all more or less like Dana, if we are honest with ourselves as we write our lists.

Since relationship is a mirror of what we are, we can see ourselves very clearly in our relationships with others, our fears and anxieties, our prejudices and griefs, our need for self-gratification and security. Since love is giving not getting, is there any loving in all this? Or only mutual self-gratification. I'll scratch your back, if you scratch mine. If a relationship lasts only as long as it is gratifying, and then it is thrown away, is there any loving in all this?

Clearly, true relationship is loving. Loving is affection without dependency, without control, without judgment, without jealousy, without possessiveness, without images of what you ought to be or what I ought to be. Clearly, the best way to understand loving, is to remember all the things it is *not*. Love is freely given, *with absolutely no expectation of returns on the dollar.* Love is a state of being, isn't it? It is responsibility for the whole earth, compassion for all human beings, not a narrow focus on a single person who happens to gratify us.

Haven't you, haven't we all, felt moments of this? A moment of a beautiful day, with the sun on your eyelids, when the grass or the hot, summer pavement smells sweet to you, and there is no pain in your body or soul? You feel connected to the whole universe, and for a moment there is an end to loneliness?

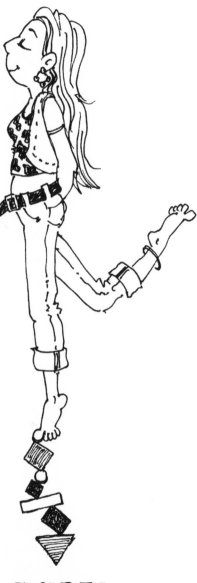

**SECURITY
IS AN
ILLUSION.**

When you are not clutching at one person, passion, or possession, you have it all.

Love and Sex

Sex is just a normal, ordinary, evolutionary act. It answers Nature's need for reproduction, our mammal need for warmth, touching, and huddling, our human need for sensory and language communication, and our psychological longing for warmth and company.

Why do we make such a fuss over it? There are at least four genders we know of, there may be more, and why do we make such a fuss over that? Reproduction is controllable, if that is the argument. Protection is available, if disease is the argument.

Back to memes, ideas that is, in our human heritage, as well as genes. Genes say sex is fine, any kind. Memes, ideas about reproduction came into fashion at about the time agriculture was invented, and made sex into a problem Nature never intended.

Hunting was a group effort, and tribes had to share both the hunting and the spoils among all tribal families. As human beings began to till fields, they wanted to own the fields they tilled and keep the food they grew for themselves and their families. Help was needed in the fields in the form of sons. Women were needed to produce those little field hands.

Men bought and sold these baby factories and were viciously protective about their women, wanting only their own seed, their own sons to inherit their land. Female virginity and virtue became valuable commodities to be bought, sold, and insisted on. So sex became a problem, particularly for women, and it was therefore scriptured, legalized, and socialized into existence.

Sex is no more a natural problem than eating, unless we make it one.

And of course, while both sex and feeding another can be expressions of love, they are certainly not love in themselves. And both, overdone or indiscriminate, can do harm to yourself and other human beings.

Friendship, Parent Love, Teacher love, Any Love

Isn't love in friendship just to be kind with no ulterior motives, just to be generous in your mind, nonjudgmental, to feel for another person?

When parents and teachers prepare children to 'fit in' to society instead of looking at themselves and society clearly, aren't they preparing people for ambition, conflict, war, and all the suffering that goes with it? After all, society is just a collection of selves, our selves, isn't it?

Society, after all, will turn out any way we turn out our children.

Can we love people without depending on them to gratify our needs?

Can we love the work we do without competition and ambition?

Can we love, work, play without having to win?

This is what it means to keep your self with its needs out of the way. Not because this is virtuous, but because if you keep your self out of the way, it can't get hurt or cause trouble. If we could just love because we love, without need for return getting in the way, we would suffer a lot less.

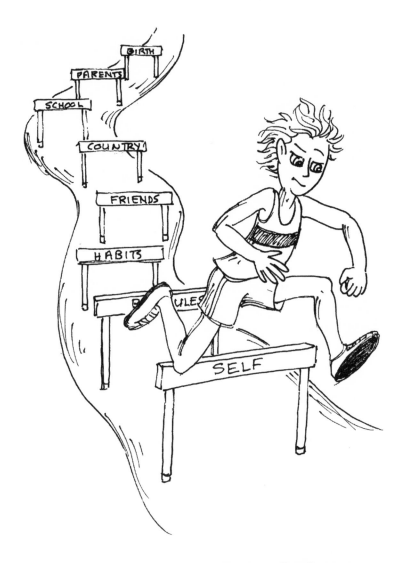

**KEEP YOUR SELF
WITH ITS NEEDS OUT
OF THE WAY.**

Look at Your Past Habits and Let Them Go

Past habits of your self in relationship will keep cropping up again and again, so again and again you have to let them go. Evolution and culture have trained us to this painful neediness, but the human brain has a marvelous capacity to change itself, to rewire itself. Unlike sheep, we don't have to go on in the same old way and huddle dumbly together as we go off a cliff.

Every time any of your relationships with people, work, sports, school, your own talents, hurt you, sit quietly somewhere and figure out what self-need got hurt. Drop the need, and go on having fun with your life.

Rules for Self

❶ Remind your brain that the struggle for importance, position as well as the desire for escape from those struggles are only the behaviors of needy selves.

❷ Remind your brain the only real needs are air to breathe, food to eat, clothes and shelter from the weather. The rest of the struggle is the impossible search for an impossible security.

❸ Don't take other selves personally. They're just running out their programming.

❹ Don't take your own self personally. Even your own personal mind-states are *mostly* the result of biological evolution (genes) and culturally conditioned ideas (memes).

❺ Remember at all times that science tells us there's no
   self anywhere inside you or your brain anyway.

❻ Most people don't know there's nobody home, no
   leader of the neuronal pack of circuits. So let down
   anybody you tell this to very gently. It comes as a
   very threatening shock to many people that self is not
   personal, that psychological thoughts and feelings
   are evolutionary brain-jerk reactions common to all
   human beings.

❼ Evolution and evolutionary neurobiology are not
   destiny. The human brain is very plastic. Change
   anything you want to change.

CHANGE

ANYTHING

YOU WANT

TO CHANGE.

Chapter Five

SELF AND EDUCATION, SCHOOL, WORK, AND MONEY

■ ■ ■

"Education must enable one to sift and weigh
evidence, to discover the true from the false, the
real from the unreal, and the facts from fiction."

—Dr. Martin Luther King, Jr., *The Maroon Tiger*

"When you get, give. When you learn, teach."

—Maya Angelou, *Collected Writings*

■ ■ ■

Why Are You Going to School?

Why are you being educated? Have you asked yourself or
anybody else why you have to spend hours every day learning
to read and write, study math and geography and history and
whatever else they are teaching you?

Why are you being crammed with all this knowledge? Just
so you can repeat the lives of your parents, work eight or ten
hours a day every week of your lives, so you can get a job, buy a
house, pay the bills to feed and educate your children—so they
can do the same thing over again?

Is that all there is to education, to repeat this struggle over and over again? What is your relationship to all this? Is it just to go through the motions to please your parents and teachers? Don't you question what learning algebra and all the rest of it is for? Whether there is any meaning in all this going to school and learning the subjects they teach you? Whether there is meaning in your life? Or do you just go through everything blindly hoping for the best—or at least to stay out of trouble.

School and Education: Intellect and Intelligence

"The right kind of education means the awakening of intelligence," said the great educator, philosopher, and teacher J. Krishnamurti in his book *Education and the Significance of Life.* "We must re-educate ourselves not to kill one another."

His point was that, along with factual information, the right kind of education must include an understanding of human beings, human brains and the mistakes they make, and where intellectual knowledge is useful, and where it is not useful.

1 Intellect is the accumulated past knowledge and skills transmitted from one generation to another.

2 Intelligence is insight, the capacity to understand where recorded information has its place, and where new eyes, new responses not based on old facts or old conditioning are called for.

Teachers are required to feed, and students are required to digest, so much information in our technologically complex world. We have all forgotten that the great importance of education is the awakening of intelligence, to teach students how to learn, and continue to learn.

Sometimes all we are taught in school is to compete for good grades to compete for good colleges to compete for good jobs to compete for everybody else's approval.

Is there a point to this?

Intellect

School instruction and memorization are only part of education. Learning to read and write, learning math, science, literature, history, social and political sciences, how to cook, farm, do carpentry, plumbing, physics, the laundry, raise children or animals, write a book, fix a car, dress hair—all this ensures you can earn a living in your particular society. This is so you can pay for your own food, clothing, shelter, taxes, and stand on your own two feet instead of someone else's. This is the necessary use of your brain's intellect. And if you are among the fortunate people on earth with enough money and position and opportunity, you can choose what you like to do with your life.

So much of life, so much time each week is given to work, that part of education is to find the interests and talent of each student. If you have to work, life is happier if you like what you are doing and have the capacity to do it well. For too many millions of people, life is just a struggle for bare subsistence, doing only work forced on them by birth and circumstances.

Intelligence

Intelligence is much greater than intellect. Intelligence is the ability to combine capability with good will instead of the usual self-centered fearful competition we live in. We all need to take the same oath doctors take—the first thing is not to do harm! To have an open mind without pre-judging the facts, without prejudice, is important both to scientists and to anyone who is an intelligent human being. The open mind is far more important than just past information. It begins with being aware of our own thoughts and feelings, our own past prejudices and knowledge. Intelligence comes through self-understanding and the observation of everyday human relationship.

Do you learn these things in school? Are there discussion groups or at least teachers with whom to discuss the meaning of education, how and why the brain works the way it does, what is the purpose of all this information beyond just getting a piece of paper at the end like a passport to the so-called real world of work, money, position, power, possessions?

Ask these questions of some parent or teacher at school so you don't go through your teens like a trained monkey! So that at the end of your life, you needn't wonder what all this effort at school, and at work, was for. If you look at the faces of older people, you'll see mostly bewilderment and pain and fatigue, because position, power, and possessions have never yet made anybody happy or fulfilled their lives. And most have never inquired why. Inquire now, for yourselves, what all the work is for. Intellect collects information. Intelligence tells you what to do with it.

INTELLIGENCE COMES THROUGH
SELF-UNDERSTANDING AND
THE OBSERVATION OF EVERYDAY
HUMAN RELATIONSHIP.

The Brain's 4 Capacities

1 **Automatic life functions.** Your brain keeps you alive. It does this mostly automatically, and keeps you breathing, balanced, coordinates sensory information to alert you to food, danger, mating opportunities, and so forth.

2 **Emotions.** This is your brain's capacity to feel all kinds of emotions, like fear, hatred, anger, jealousy as well as joy, pleasure, affection, sympathy, warmth, etc. Emotions are the driving energies of your life. They make you think and act in certain ways.

3 **Intellect.** This is your brain's capacity to collect new information, hold it in the form of memory, remember it when necessary and think, learn from that memory. Intellect guides your actions.

4 **Intelligence.** This is your brain's capacity to read in between the lines, i.e. to understand not only the obvious, the visible but also the subtle, the hidden. This capacity is required for understanding yourself, what to do, how to live life without harm—so your life can matter, to yourself, to others, to the world.

The first three capacities are fairly evolved in human beings, while the fourth capacity is still largely undeveloped.

Who Is Responsible for Your Education?

The usual answer is both school and your parents at home.

The further answer in this book is **you!**

Only *you* live inside your skin, only *you* live behind your own eyes, only *you* can look into your own brain, only *you* are in charge of your own self-understanding, your own behavior. Only *you* can live your own life.

So self-knowledge, and therefore the understanding of everyone else (remember we all have pretty much the same human selves) is the other part of education. Without understanding that your self, and everyone else's, is a prison from which escape through understanding is absolutely necessary—we are all doomed to go through our lives acting like angry convicts in the prisons of our selves, banging everyone else over the head to get what we want.

You don't have to join the psychological chain gang of most of humanity. Learn the human race's information at school and at home—there's no need to reinvent the wheel, brain surgery, or baseball—and with your new understanding in this book of the psychological structure of the human self, stand on your own two psychological feet.

In other words, take the technical information they give you. Then decide what to do with it yourself in order to live a meaningful life, a humane, not just a human animal, life. This means to live with intelligence, not to be afraid all the time, of failure, of other people's opinions, of not being liked or approved of or not belonging.

Competition, Ambition, Getting Ahead—or Cooperation

Sadly, the major lesson students are taught, at home as well as in school, is to compete instead of cooperate. Winning, being someone important, getting ahead of the crowd. Of course, it is necessary as an adult to earn money if you can so you can take care of yourself, perhaps others—otherwise you become a burden and someone else has to take care of you. But isn't the first thing about being truly human not to harm yourself or another while you live and make a living?

We live on an abundant planet. Typhoons, floods and drought, volcanic eruptions and just plain bad luck happen. But think what the world would be like if we cooperated and shared, instead of adding to natural disasters by murdering each other and maiming our children in wars. Instead of the divisive nature of nationalism, what if we organized a world economy so that people got what they needed instead of having to fight for everything from luxuries to barely enough to eat. This isn't a moral lecture, or a passport to some theoretical heaven. This is simply the practical way to limit people's suffering, to cooperate instead of kill each other for what we need.

Why, instead, are we taught fear? Aren't you fearful when a teacher or parent criticizes you? When you get a bad mark, or you are bullied by others, or you are afraid of not having enough of something? Why don't we get taught the causes of fear in the human brain, both evolutionarily and in our personal lives, and how to handle that fear and overcome it? True education helps you to understand life, not just scramble for a security that never exists, and the boredom and unhappiness of previous generations.

Your Relationship to School, Work, Money

What is your relationship to school? What are you like in school in relationship to:

❶ Cliques, gangs, the particular group you belong to? Do you lead or follow? Do you dominate or depend on others? What are your motives for being either dependent or controlling? Do you gossip for a feeling of power? Do you use physical measures to assure your place in the clique, such as money, favors, drugs, sex, mental or physical bullying? Can you examine why you do these things?

❷ Teachers? What is your relationship to your teachers? Do you compete, act out, work hard for their approval? Do you like or fear any of your teachers?

❸ Classes? How do you behave in class when you like the subject and teacher? How do you behave when you don't like class? Do you put up and shut up? Do you ask to talk to your teachers when you have a problem with the subject, the teacher, the teaching method? Are you encouraged to discover your interests and talents, what you like to do, what you would like to do for work, with your life? If not at school, at home? If nowhere, can you discover for yourself what work you want to do in your life, what interests you? Do you know how to ask for help in thinking all these things out?

4 Sports? Do you compete to win? Do you compete for the fun of it? What are your feelings when you win? Lose? How do you handle them? What do your schools, your parents say about winning and losing? Do you agree with them?

5 Do you like or not like school? Why? Do you like or not like the people in it? Why?

6 Do you think marks are important—not because your parents and teachers tell you so, but you yourself?

7 Do you have a paying job after school? For what purpose? Do you agree with the purpose? Do you like the work? Is anyone teaching you that it is important to love what you do for the work itself, without ambition connected to the work? Ambition may always return to get in the way, but each time it does, can you again separate out the love of your work from the rewards, which only breed more disappointment, self-hate, anger, and fear than the short-lived pleasure they give? Again, none of this is meant as a moral lecture. It is only a happier, less fearful way to live your life.

8 Can you now answer the question: what is education for? Are we being brought up to be killed, either in war, or for the sake of competition, or in the work force from sheer boredom, living meaningless lives as so many of our parents and grandparents did? The goal of life surely is joy in living, both given and received, not the repetition of pain from generation to generation.

Physical Pain, Mental Suffering

Obviously there is physical suffering. All people need food, clothing, shelter, and many people in many countries face physical crises. Physical pain comes along with having a physical body. Mental suffering (unless you have a biochemical mental disease such as schizophrenia or depression) is not necessary. When you understand and get over the illusion of your self, intense psychological suffering disappears.

Why Aren't We Told About this Well-Kept Secret?

This understanding of the self, yourself, obviously begins with education. From nursery school to doctorate, education must change its emphasis from destructive competition to helpful cooperation. We must be taught from the beginning that we are not separate selves.

My friend Mark Lee told me of a student/teacher dialogue at the Oak Grove High School in Ojai, California about this whole problem of teaching young people about the self. One of the teen students asked the most important question of all.

Student: *Why do teachers and parents and other adults tell us we each have this precious little self when we are small, if it isn't true? Why teach us this hoax when, once you believe in the idea of self, it's so hard to get rid of? Why not tell us from the beginning that our sense of having a self is just constructed by thought? It's so hard in our teens to undo the idea of having a self after so many years.*

Teacher: *You've asked the best question in human culture. And the answers are sad. The first response I have is that most parents, teachers, and other educators have never taken the time to investigate this illusion that we each have a separate self. Most don't know since they've never thought about it. My second response is that, because while learning about yourselves may be in your best interest, it may serve others who want to control you to keep you ignorant. If you think you have a self that needs to be secure, to be loved, to win awards, ultimately to go to heaven, it is much easier to make you behave, to sell you things and ideas, to make you pick up an explosive and kill. Ignorance and control are the two major factors in why many adults keep the great secret that we're not separate, each out for herself or himself, but that we're all in this together.*

Whoever Understands Must Help
Change Our Evolutionary Heritage

Humans are a social, herd, pack animal. Our curiosity to learn new things, our need to work, to contribute, to be valuable is a matter of survival. It is hard-wired into the nerve pathways of our brains. This is not only to get our daily bread, but so that we will be valued by the pack, and not left out in the rain to die.

But we have technology, we have world communication capacities, we have supermarkets now.

We don't have to be competitive killers to drink at the waterhole with the other animals anymore. So we need to look at why we continue to compete for everything. We need to educate ourselves and our young to celebrate life instead of just endure.

People with few opportunities must work where they can, but even they can discover what they like to do and the joy of creating their own inner lives.

Old Patterns or New Freedoms

■ ■

"To find out what you love to do demands a great deal of intelligence; because, if you are afraid of not being able to earn a livelihood, or of not fitting into this rotten society, then you will never find out. But, if you are not frightened, if you refuse to be pushed into the groove of tradition by your parents, your teachers, by the superficial demands of society, then there is a possibility of discovering what it is you really love to do. So, to discover, there must be no fear of not surviving."

J. Krishnamurti, *What Are You Doing with Your Life?*

■ ■

Chapter Six

SELF AND PARENTS, FAMILY, CULTURE, COUNTRY, WORLD

■ ■ ■

"Can parents claim to love their children when, by educating them wrongly, they foster envy, enmity, and ambition? Is it love that stimulates the national and racial antagonisms which lead to war, destruction and utter misery, that sets man against man in the name of religions and ideologies?"

— J. Krishnamurti, *Relationships: To Oneself, To Others, To the World*

"When the individual families have learned kindness, then the whole nation has learned kindness."

— Confucius, *Ethics and Politics, VII*

■ ■ ■

Can Families be Open and Connected, not Closed and Exclusive?

A family could be in loving relationship to all human existence, not an enclosed system that is exclusive, separative, and divisive like nations, religions, and tribes.

Most families behave like tanks in a war zone, enclosing a few against the many, with its attitudes cocked and ready to criticize, dislike, fear, feel superior to or suspicious of—or even just exclude non-family. There is no love in this, only war.

Neighborhoods, like gangs and cliques, are the outgrowth of family. Tribes and nations and religions are the expression of neighborhoods.

Groups Could Cooperate instead of Grab

We could learn that all groupings of people are for cooperative support, not for grabbing what other people have or for controlling their ideas or their behavior. Of course, for this to happen, we have to look at the whole business of 'I' and 'mine', my property, my bank account, my identity and ideas, my security. This is very, very hard, perhaps the hardest job there is. But if I am not willing to give up my ideas of physical and emotional security, how can I expect you or anyone else to give up theirs?

The Need to Belong, to Nurture, and to Be Nurtured

These needs have an evolutionary source. From people to penguins, according to the neuroscientist Jaak Panksepp, our brains secrete two hormones called oxytocin and vasopressin that cause parents to feed, nurture, teach, and protect their young from harm. These chemicals make parents willing to sacrifice for their young, feed their young even if it means hunger for themselves, protect their young at the risk of their own lives if necessary.

These nurturing hormones are part of life's genetic instructions for the survival of life through reproduction.

Evolutionary Source of Family and National War

Almost all physically capable life will threaten, fight, and kill to save themselves, their families, their mates, their young. Nature insists. The cardinal law of life is to go on living. Flight, or aggressive response to fear or actual attack, is our evolutionary inheritance, bred into every cell, every nerve, muscle, bone, every organ from belly to brain.

The fact of this evolutionary command has to be stressed in order to understand how hard it is to overcome these family, tribal, national instincts.

The trouble is, what worked during the last ice age when we lived in small bands in caves and each family or band had to fight over an animal for dinner, *does not work any more.* Our killing weapons have become too powerful. And it's hard enough fighting floods, famine, and other natural disasters, without fighting each other.

Evolutionary Cure for Family Fights and National War

But evolutionary nature gave us another tool, a tool that has the capacity to moderate our instinctive behavior.

Other animals do not have our frontal lobes to understand their natures and decide on whether their instinctive responses are appropriate. Humans do.

Complex human brains, as we have said, have the capacity not only for intellect, which is thought and feelings, but also for intelligence, which is understanding of what is actually going on!

We can see that neither genes nor social conditioning need dictate our behavior. Just because somebody gives you a gun, doesn't mean you have to use it. Just because somebody tells

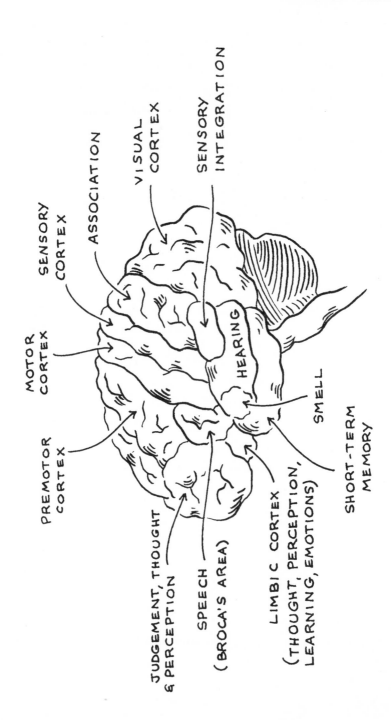

you to fight another country, family, or gang, doesn't mean you have to do it.

Fear and anger happen. Mentally and emotionally taking sides happens. Our evolutionary brain circuits are programmed for these feelings and reactions.

We can reprogram our brains and the behavior they dictate any time. With intelligence. With mutational insight. Changing behavior changes and reprograms the brain's neural paths and connections. Let reactions pass before acting.

Families, like Nationality, Color, Noses, Are an Accident of Birth

You may not like your relatives. You don't get to choose them as you choose your friends.

But just because you are stuck with your family (until you can pay your own bills) does not mean you have to treat them worse than anyone else. *You don't have to like people in order to be kind and get along with them.* And this is for your own sake, not for theirs. How many nights have you been awake and all twisted up inside with rage or fear, while whomever you're upset with has been having a good night's sleep? How many times have you been punished for being rude, when all you had to do was keep your mouth shut no matter what you were thinking? Kindness pays, whether you feel kind or not. Remember, a feeling does not have to be a wild horse that drags you down blind alleys. You actually can have a feeling and shut up about it. This was news to me when I learned it as a forty-something adult, so I repeat it. I always thought if I had feelings, I had to express them or act on them.

- You don't have to like people if they are not likeable, only be kind emotionally as well as physically.

- You don't have to honor people, including teachers and parents, if they are not honorable.

- You don't even, if you are a save-the-world type, have to fix them, correct their ideas and behavior, or save them. You don't even have to like people to get along with them.

- You DO have to, as pledged in the oath doctors take, DO NO HARM to them or yourself. This does not mean play along to get along. You do not have to dishonor yourself.

- You can just shut up, behave yourself, walk away.

What to Do Instead of Making a Mental, Verbal, or Actual Fist

Pay attention to the violence rising in you. Blood may rush to your head. You may feel your adrenalin run through your body, your heartbeat quicken. You may sweat, your face may turn red, your eyes burn, your hands may clench, your stomach may tighten, your breathing quicken. Do nothing, say nothing, just be aware of anger symptoms in your own body.

Be Aware of Evolutionary Animal Nature

Remember we are animals. And animals feel threatened by confrontation, whether that's someone getting in our face, growls, or in our case, using hurtful or angry words. Animals often threaten rather than kill each other when confronted, with noises, physical stances and threatening ground or chest-beating. We could learn this from them.

What Do You Do When You Are Confronted?

Among human animal response choices:

1 Shout back out loud.

2 Argue in your head.

3 Go along. Submit in fear.

4 Worry over being unpopular or unloved if you disagree.

5 Put up a wall, act as if you don't care.

6 Somatize, convert mental distress to physical symptoms like getting a stomach ache or headache or breaking your own leg from the distress.

7 Escape into sex, drugs, alcohol, shopping, television, an iPod, Internet, games, books, whatever.

8 Intellectualize to avoid feeling the emotional reaction
with who is right, who is wrong. (This can go on for
decades, long after the original argument or hurt.)

9 Kill, by word or action, stonewalling or stoning, gossip
or guns.

EXPERIMENT: Don't Just Do Something, Stand There
The next time a family member, teacher, or friend criticizes or
confronts you, or the family, school team, country, or the next
time a religious, cultural, color group takes sides, and you
have strong, brain-jerk, reactive feelings—do and say nothing.
Breathe deeply. Leave a gap, a moment of space before you

EXPERIMENT
The next time a family
member, teacher, friend
confronts you, and you
feel pain or anger—
breathe deeply and do
nothing. Don't add fuel
to your fire, the fire will
die instead of burn you.

do anything in response. Your anger and pain will dissolve if you don't add fuel to the fire with your own habitual words and actions in confrontations. Just try this and see if there is a difference in your behavior. You may find you can choose an appropriate response, instead of just reacting to someone else's words or behavior. This intelligence gives you freedom both from them and your conditioned 'self.'

What Are You Like in Groups?

There are always arguments, confrontations, sides taken, different views expressed. What are your thoughts and behaviors like when other people's ideas conflict with your own?

At the family dinner table

In school groups, classroom or social or sports

At community places like church, temple, mosque, scouts, social or political gatherings

In your own clique or gang get-togethers

- Do you argue? Fight as if your survival was at stake?
- Smolder?
- Play divide and conquer?
- Do you moderate? Question and invite dialogue?
- Take sides?
- Do you feel everyone has to like you and play for popularity?
- Do you feel you have to be right? Why?

Take the Pressure off Feeling Animal
Threat with Human Intelligence

We no longer have to fight for the water hole. With modern technology and transportation, there is plenty to go around if we share instead of fight, or at least remember that there is always another water hole.

Most important is to have a global mind, not a petty personal mind. So, with such a global mind, how do you look at a family, a country, a group, a culture? What is your relationship to your family? What is your relationship to your country? Will you kill? Will you separate yourself from other families, people in other countries? Can you remain global no matter what?

Like it or not, perceive it or not, we are all in this together. Cosmologists say thirteen billion years ago, the condensed ball of all matter in the universe exploded into the particles we and everything else are made of, connected by universal forces like gravity. And here we all are—collections of those same particles and forces, all part of the universe and all connected. It would be far less lonely and far more honest to see this truth, that all people are family, the whole earth is home, that we are all particles of the whole universe.

If your eyes are blinded with worries about yourself, your own ideas, status, power, pleasures, and position, you cannot see the freeing truth that you are exactly like the people you are standing next to, and they are exactly like you. Why not understand instead of fight?

Self-Consciousness

Many forms of life are conscious. Humans are self-conscious—conscious of being conscious. We therefore must become scientists of that self we are so aware of, and watch that self closely.

As we have noticed, we have no separate existence from everything else, so whatever goes around comes around. Punch people's faces, they'll be mad enough to punch another face, and sooner or later, it comes back to you and your own nose gets broken. In the East, this is called *karma*. In the West, we call this *cause and effect*. All acts have consequences.

It's not that we won't go on making mistakes. But we can correct these mistakes as we go along, make them right, and resume watching our selves and what we are doing and saying.

Chapter Seven

SELF, SOCIETY AND AUTHORITY

■ ■ ■

"Those who would take over the earth
And shape it to their will
Never, I notice, succeed."

— Lao Tzu, *The Way of Life, 29*

"Everything is determined...by forces over which
we have no control. It is determined for the
insect as well as the star. Human beings, vegetables,
or cosmic dust—we all dance to a mysterious tune,
intoned in the distance by an invisible piper."

— Albert Einstein, *The Saturday Evening Post, 1929*

■ ■ ■

Isn't it Fear and the Need for Security that Make You Obey?

We are discussing in this book the awakening of your own intelligence. So that you do not live your life meaninglessly as society's robot, according to someone else's rules. Life can be deadly dull if all you do is follow other people's blueprints. It can be equally deadly if all you do is argue just for the sake of rebelling. That way you just become a negative blueprint. Both ways you live without freedom in a psychological prison. Life is only really *alive* if you write your own script.

This does not mean you do exactly as you please. You'll go to jail if you break laws, deal drugs, carry a gun. You'll face punishment if you ignore school regulations or the rules of the house at home.

Evolutionary Background for Obedience

Our mammal upbringing has been based on "tell me what to do."

If a mother lion does not teach her cub how to be safe, it will be killed. If a mother gorilla does not teach her baby what leaves to eat, it will starve. This behavior is encoded in their genes.

But humans teach their children more than genetic information. We teach and pass on ideas, memes, embedded in our culture, especially the idea of self, that each of us has an actual self.

Note: Just because something has been said, an idea has been repeated for thousands of years, doesn't make it right. Until pretty recently, people thought *and told their children,* that the Earth was flat and the sun revolved around us. *It just felt that way, until science proved otherwise.*

By the same token, it *feels* as if we have a self. Science proves otherwise.

But humans go on teaching their children they have a self. Only the trouble with the self, as we have discovered, is that self is greedy. To feel safe, it always wants *more*. Wanting more, being taught to compete for more, growing addicted to more of everything all the time, leads to being unhappy for all of your life. And we teach human children always to want, to compete for more, and to live forever with those conflicted voices in our heads (I'm not good enough, must try harder, get more glory, position, power, possessions, beat the other guy for security).

Intelligence knows when enough is enough, but there is almost no modeling, no power of example, for this.

So we accept authority, and live in mental prisons in order to be safe instead of free.

> *Can you, therefore, obey society's legal rules and*
> *still not obey, not accept, its ideas about what*
> *is important or how to live your life?*

Can you, instead of living in the perpetual conflict of getting somewhere (where?) and getting stuff (how much is enough?) stop measuring yourself against everyone else and live your life the way you want to live it, do work you love to do, not just for money, marry someone you really like and not for someone else's reasons?

Freedom Is not Safe

It doesn't feel safe living according to your own independent light, in psychological freedom.

It feels safer following your family's rules and society's plans for you.

YOU ARE SAFE ONLY WHEN YOU ARE DEAD. AT LEAST, LIVE FIRST!

But ask yourself some questions:

1 Are you willing to marry and be lonely the rest of your life?

2 Are you willing to murder a child if your country gives you a gun?

3 Are you willing to be bored in an office if you don't like offices, or on a farm if you don't like farming?

4 Are you willing to do as you are told for money?

We end up accepting authority to be safe, if we aren't careful. But you are safe only when you are dead.

At least, *live first!*

And beware: adults tend to tell you how to live only partly to protect you and help you and the human race to survive. Adults also tend to tell you what to do to validate themselves and their own way of living life.

Which does not mean, throw out everything you hear.

Some of it may be right on.

Factual Authority Is One Thing:
Psychological Authority is Another

So, as we see, humans have a habit of telling each other what to do, partly out of care-taking, partly out of culture-preservation or self-importance. Keep in mind always that the self is just the sum of our memories, not a pipeline to the truth. We are the nerds with brains who invent self-importance as a survival tool, as other creatures have fur or claws. If you do as I do, believe what I believe, it makes me important, says your brain.

Or as psychologist Steven Pinker says in his book *How the Mind Works*, "The brain and the [elephant's] trunk are products of the same evolutionary force...We are chauvinistic about our brains, thinking them to be the goal of evolution. And that makes no sense, for reasons articulated...by [scientist] Stephen Jay Gould (who says we are only a twig somewhere on the bush of life, not the top of its tree). Natural selection does nothing even close to striving for intelligence."

Intelligence may, indeed, exist outside the human brain, not in it, and what we need to do is be quiet so it can come to us as insight, or inspiration.

Intelligence, Sensitivity to the Truth, Is What We are After

My respect for young people lies in their search for the truth, the need for understanding in the midst of confusion. Pain makes many adults glaze over the questions of life, why are we living, why do we hurt, and bury themselves in busyness and old answers that haven't worked for ten thousand years.

Too much pain can make people insensitive. Sensitivity is not the same as self-protective touchiness. Sensitivity is being aware of others, all society and people, of nature, of the whole of the universe. Webster's *New Collegiate Dictionary* defines sensitivity as 'delicately aware of the attitudes and feelings of others.'

WE ARE ONLY A TWIG
SOMEWHERE ON THE
BUSH OF LIFE.

Inner War and Conflict Create
Outer War and Conflict

"What you are, society is," says Krishnamurti. Each of us is what makes up society, after all, so society cannot be anything other than what we all are. Our warring inner selves produce outer wars. Listen to the voices arguing in your head.

The brain, all three parts, old dinosaur brain in back, animal brain in the middle, human frontal cortex, have recorded all the parental voices from your childhood. These of course are their parents' voices and all the parents, of mammals, reptiles, fish, and amoeba before them. These billions of years of inherited survival-directed voices produce the anger and fear in us that we take out on everybody else.

By paying attention to these inner voices, ancient echoes as well as the current authority and prejudices, opinions, and painful experiences of your mother, your father, a teacher, you can end them if they make no sense. An example of these survival-directed voices might be 'you're not good enough yet' or 'you're entitled to the best.' Either way, you come out fighting.

There Must Be No Psychological Authority

There must be no psychological authority in the search for life's meaning, for whether there is God, or how to live. You must discover all this for yourself. Obviously, we obey rules about courtesy, traffic, safety. Freedom from authority does not mean freedom to do whatever we like. Freedom does not mean you can just do as you please, regardless of its effect. Freedom also includes responsibility—for yourself, for everyone everywhere, even for the Earth itself to keep it from being destroyed so you and everybody else has a place to live.

Because each human brain has created a self out of its thoughts, memories, out of our personal stories and evolutionary histories, we all share exactly the same myths and habits of protecting these nonexistent selves.

So don't let that self and its instincts either run wild or be controlled by others' reins. Just because other people's selves are either out of control or living in terror from fear and greed, doesn't mean you have to live that way. Don't be afraid to be the only one in your crowd or family to understand the phantom psychological structure of the self. You will find friends here and there all over the world who have discovered or who are discovering the truth as well.

Remember the story of the little boy who saw that the Emperor had been fooled by his courtiers into thinking he was wearing a new suit of golden clothes, when in fact he was naked? Only one little boy refused to lie about what he saw and went around shouting the truth. Well, he may have been alone. But he was right.

So Watch It

Watch as your self comes and goes, talks to you when you are not occupied, seems to disappear when you are busy. Watch it. Observe it. Use your intelligence, your compassion for yourself and everybody else to direct your life in society, to live your life with meaning instead of boredom, be happy instead of in pain.

EXPERIMENT: What Are the Rules in Your Life?

Besides 'don't play in traffic', list some of the major rules in your life you have been told to obey or get into trouble.

Home	*School*	*Social*
clean room	*do homework*	*no drugs, no guns*
be on time	*no fighting*	*win at sports*
family comes first	*compete for marks*	*no sex*

These rules give you an idea of what your society considers good and bad behavior. Do you agree or disagree with them? Why? Do have a group of friends with whom you can discuss these matters? Your own lists will be a lot longer than those above. Go into your culture's expectations of you at home, school, in terms of your country, your nationality, your religion. See what you are up against. What is important to remember here is that there is a world of difference between goodboyism and goodgirlism (just fitting in, turning into society's robots) and living rightly as a human being. Decide for yourself, for instance, whether getting enough food to eat is good for everyone and murder in the form of patriotism and gang loyalty or competition instead of cooperation may not be good for everyone.

Examine society's rules for yourself. Don't just copy behavior to play it safe. Society's rules for behavior, from work to war to marriage, could cripple you for life.

Chapter Eight

SELF AND NATURE, ANIMALS, THE EARTH

■ ■ ■

"Animals are not ours to eat, wear, experiment
on, or use for our entertainment."

— People for the Ethical Treatment of Animals, Sticker

"Animals are other nations…What is man without the
beasts? If all the beasts were gone, men would die from
great loneliness of spirit, for whatever happens to the
beasts also happens to man. All things are connected."

— Chief Seattle, Speech, 1853

■ ■ ■

What Is Your Relationship to Nature?
Go somewhere and look at a tree. Tilt your head back and look
at the sky, at the shapes of clouds as they move across the sky.
Look at anything not man-made, anything in nature. Just look,
really look. We are so full of thoughts, ideas, opinions, to-do
lists, nervous anxieties about ourselves, we miss our whole
relationship to the earth we're standing on, to the sky above
us, to the vast universe we live in. We forget that the grass, the
cats, and the cows, as well as ourselves, are all made of the same
elements, out of stardust.

Our loneliness, our feelings of isolation from the rest of nature, are just an illusion of separation, not a fact. The heart of an elephant beats just like your own.

Raise your hand. Touch a leaf. Pat the air. All the same, elementally.

Can We Use the Earth without Abuse?

We can use our planet without murdering everything on it. Earth will go on regenerating for billions of years until our star the Sun expands and burns us up. Presumably, because we are such technologically talented primates, by then we will have found a way to transport ourselves to other worlds.

The thing is, we have to stay alive until then. This means not only understanding ourselves so that we can harness our natural instincts, but understanding our relationship to the natural world so we don't kill off what supports us. It is not a matter of being good *of* us, but good *for* us.

Just as we often use people without having a relationship with them, we use the Earth—we don't have a *relationship* with it.

We need to learn to be intelligent, not just clever. We need to love the Earth, understand it, not just use it.

Not a Biology Course

It is always possible to learn a lot of facts, about rocks and trees, the formations of mountains, about the insides of mammals, and the dinosaur origins of birds.

What we must also learn is the beauty of Earth, its courage, its tenderness. Go for a walk in a city street, where against all probability a bit of grass pushes itself up through a crack in the pavement, a soot-covered tree, thin, starved, lifts its branches to find a ray of sunlight, a bedraggled potted flower on a fire-escape or a windowsill plant manage somehow to stay alive. A cat or a dog here, a cow or pig or buffalo in another country, snuffle for street scraps and keep on breathing. If you have the luxury of living where life has green spaces, trees, water, endless sky, go out into it. Go by yourself. Turn your eyes into windows, looking out, not mirrors in which you still peer anxiously at yourself. Look at everything out there you can see. Nature is luxuriant, you will notice. There is enough for all of us, and will be, if we don't abuse it.

Part of our abuse is to say, this is mine, that is yours. Of course, we buy land, cultivate it, put a house on it, to take shelter and raise our young. But this is a convention, not a fact. The Earth is ours, not yours or mine, American or European or African or Asian. The pictures the astronauts took of our blue Earth shining in space had no country's boundary lines, no personal property lines drawn on it.

We have lost our sense of beauty and belonging to the Earth in our escape into technology, information-gathering, social acceptance games, political power activity.

We have lost our connection with animals in our rush to eat and own them, take over their lands, train them to obey or entertain us, work for us, be our surrogates in laboratory experiments. As if they were things, objects, without lives and loves of their own.

Nature and Human Self-Importance

We have separated ourselves from nature, partly because it scares us (all that thunder, lightning, all those tsunamis and tornadoes) and partly because, out of that fear, we want to dominate it and control it. And we have grown addicted to ourselves, to our own self-importance.

No wonder human beings feel so lost and alone and disconnected.

But because we have done this to ourselves, we can undo this ourselves. If we have lost our way, we can find it again.

So many writers, artists, film-makers, scientists, religious leaders are busy inventing new worlds. When there isn't a thing wrong with this one, if we could just stop spitting on it long enough to love it, care for it, nurture it.

It may be only human to behave like a clever animal, but I say, as always, it's time to graduate from human to humane.

Ask Your Self Some Questions

1 What is your relationship with animals?

Do you take care of any?

Do you eat any?

When you see a hurt or hungry stray or lost animal, do you stop and help?

Do you respect all animal species enough to protest inhumane treatment like caging them in zoos or on farms, experimenting on them in laboratories, wearing their skins and fur when fake copies or other materials would keep you just as covered and warm?

Do you sometimes stop your life to watch the flight of birds? The little nations of ant hills? The nests of rabbits or mice? Even just connecting your eyes, your senses with a tree, the sky over you, will return you to the arms of the universe.

2 What is your relationship to litter?

Do you pick it up only in your own yard or school?

Do you pick it up anywhere you see it, everywhere you go because you have a global mind?

3 Do you have a self-involved brain about our planet and use anything you please, or are you concerned about Earth's resources and use only what you need?

4 Do you sometimes pause to feel sunlight on your face or rain, or the cool earth or the hot pavement under your feet? It can ground you, to feel where you belong, to know that you belong, that it is your Earth, too.

5 Can you tell the difference between what things the insecure, frightened, often lonely and sometimes desperately unhappy self of you wants for escape or comfort—and what you really need in your life? This doesn't mean don't treat yourself or ask for what you want, but can you just be aware of the difference?

"When You Get, Give"—Maya Angelou

Whenever you, or your family or friends, feel a craving for something you do not actually need, question in your mind

DO YOU HAVE
A GLOBAL MIND?

what self-gratification, pleasure, power or position displays—or even just unthinking habit—are involved. Use your intelligence, your awareness, to distinguish the motives behind conspicuous consumption. It is not necessary to deny desire. Just be aware that collecting things will never fill the empty hole inside you. Strangely, only giving, not getting, fills that hole.

Killing Animals, the Earth, and Each Other

In *Relationships: To Oneself, To Others, To the World*, J. Krishnamurti wrote: "The problem is that of killing, and not merely killing animals for food. A man is not virtuous because he doesn't eat meat, nor is he any less virtuous because he does...

There are many forms of killing, are there not? There is killing by a word or a gesture, killing in fear or in anger, killing for a country or an ideology, killing for a set of economic dogmas or religious beliefs...

With a word or a gesture you may kill a man's reputation; through gossip, defamation, contempt, you may wipe him out. And does not comparison kill? Don't you kill a boy by comparing him with another who is cleverer or more skillful? A man who kills out of hate or anger is regarded as a criminal and put to death. Yet the man who deliberately bombs thousands of people off the face of the earth in the name of his country is honored, decorated; looked upon as a hero. Killing is spreading over the earth. For the safety or expansion of one nation, another is destroyed...

So the issue we are discussing is not merely the killing or the non-killing of animals, but the cruelty and hate that are ever increasing in the world and in each one of us. That is our real problem, isn't it?"

Chapter Nine

SELF AND GOD, THE UNIVERSE, THE UNKNOWN

■ ■ ■

"Something unknown is doing we don't know what."

— Sir Arthur Eddington, *Science and the Unseen World*

"A moment. The moment of orgasm. The moment
by the ocean when there is just the wave. The moment
of being in love. The moment of crisis when we forget
ourselves and do just what is needed…These
moments appear again and again in our lives…
This glimpse reveals to the person that there is
something more…when you "forget yourself."

— Ram Dass (Richard Alpert), *The Journey of Awakening*

■ ■ ■

**We Have All Had Moments Connected to the Universe, by
Whatever Name You Call WHAT Is Beyond, Behind, Eternal.**

Evolution and Universal Consciousness

I sent my friend and co-author the physicist Kishore Khairnar the following question.

"What is evolutionary success? By what standard do we judge evolutionary success?" Evolutionary scientist Stephen Jay Gould discusses this question in his book *Full House*. Gould's view is that evolution is not a ladder of progress, but a bush with many branches, a celebration of diversity. He says that if we are going to judge by numerical success, we live in the Age of Bacteria, not humans. If we are to judge by diversity, the category of 'bony fishes' constitutes the greatest variety of species. And if we are to judge by longevity, the microbe wins. His point is to remove human arrogance about our own evolutionary importance. He questions whether the human brain is any more miraculous an evolutionary development than the elephant's trunk or a bat's sonar. Just because we have decided human intellect is the most important of qualities doesn't make it so, and may in fact be the cause of our imminent extinction.

Kishore's response to my inquiry was the following:

"A very interesting question indeed. But the answer is very simple. The standard for success in evolution will depend on what you consider as *evolved*. Is it the evolving biological form you consider important, or is it the consciousness that has evolved as a result of the biological form. It is in the human brain that consciousness has evolved. It is the human brain that provides a better instrument for consciousness to manifest."

Kishore adds:

"Human consciousness has evolved in terms of its information. In non-human species, information is gathered only through interaction with the environment. This information is nothing but the knowledge necessary for security.

In humans, information is also generated through the thinking process. So we not only gather knowledge from the environment, we change the environment through our knowledge. This technological knowledge we call useful, and it goes on evolving.

"However, we also generate a lot of not-so-useful knowledge—psychological fear, anger, pleasure, hatred, jealousy, violence. These are not going to evolve slowly into their opposite. We can only end them each time they arise in us through insight into their nature."

Humans have the capacity to change their consciousnesses spontaneously. We may be a great evolutionary success. But this makes us less innocent than other animals when we destroy, more culpable when we hurt, more responsible for the earth and the universe, it seems to me, than other creatures who are not aware of their actions and feelings, or capable of changing their behavior.

Are We the Consciousness of the Universe?

Scientist Rupert Sheldrake's biological experiments with rats proved that rats share a common consciousness. He taught a trick to one group of rats in Australia. And the next generation of the same species of rat in Hong Kong, New Delhi, Tokyo, Moscow, and New York learned the trick much faster These experiments seem to prove that rats as well as humans as a species share a common consciousness. Learning in one member of a species

DO WE SHARE THE COSMIC
CONSCIOUSNESS?

affects the whole species. Since humans, just like the rats, share a consciousness as Bohm, Torey, Khairnar, and other physicists and philosophers, research biologists, and neuroscientists suggest, everything you are and do, even think and feel, may be passed on to everyone else.

Do We Share the Cosmic Consciousness?

The conscious mind here and in other parts of the universe may be, if we don't use it for destruction, a shared, common positive force. This shared consciousness could be the force that eventually reverses the universe's entropy, its death and eventual collapse. A shared consciousness could play an active role in the cosmic drama in the restoration of the future of the life of the universe.

Human consciousness, then, may be not just global, but cosmic, universal, affecting with its thoughts, behaviors, emotions, all the particles of the universe. Think about *that* sentence whenever you wonder if you matter or not! Quantum physics itself supports this: it is the observer that affects the outcome of whatever it observes, even whether, for instance, light is a wave or a particle. Human observation determines what it sees. If human consciousness affects the properties of light and shapes and colors, why not everything else?

So, What Do You Think?

❶ Are we just one passing species among many, a twig on the diverse bush of life and not the star at the top of the life's tree? Is this really the Age of Bacteria, not Homo Sapiens?

2 Are we the Consciousness of the Universe, with an effect on the entire fate of the Cosmos, capable of eventually understanding the Theory of Everything? This is a scientific question, but it's here that Physics and Metaphysics become one. Or as the great Stephen Hawking says, to understand the answer to this is to understand the Mind of God.

Are We Hardwired for God?

Why are humans obsessed with God, whatever we all personally, culturally, religiously call God? Animal scientist Temple Grandin says humans, and possibly all animals, seem to be hardwired physically and neuronally, for religious feeling, a sense of awe and magic.

What has science to say about the origin of religion? The purpose of physical life is to stay alive. Everything that moves needs something like a mind to stay out of harm's way. Even a clam has a harm-detector in its foot. As Dennett points out in his book about the evolution of religion (*Breaking the Spell: Religion as a Natural Phenomenon*), the human brain is more complex than the foot of a clam. We attribute a hidden agency to anything that moves or rustles in the leaves. "The false alarms generated by our overactive disposition to look for agents are the irritants around which the pearls of religion grow." Clearly, there is something sacred in the universe. We all sense it. And we can't resist trying to describe it.

Religion also survives because it is a group-bonding and therefore a survival tool. Group belief, group stories, keeps people together, huddled in the dark, bonded for security.

What is this yearning, this search for God we can trace in our own species as far back as Cro-Magnon cave-dwellers, through their cave art and ritual artifact remains? Is there a Spirit of the Universe pressing us to find itself? Are we searching in the dark universe out of our own suffering, loneliness, and sense of confusion and incompleteness, for God as mother/father, security? Are we searching for the answers to questions like why is life such a struggle, is there meaning?

The brain and body cells are so interconnected, that it is the whole organism yearning for connection, not just a particular brain system. Individual consciousness, says Khairnar, is self-centered and therefore limited. This limitation expresses itself in the form of a feeling of inadequacy, and it is out of this feeling that the human being seeks completeness. And this search for completeness is the yearning to connect with something that is greater, nobler than itself.

The feeling of inadequacy is due to this self-centeredness and to our lack of understanding ourselves. As long as we mistakenly insist that we are each a separate self, we can never have self-knowledge. But if we understand the self is only illusion and not really there, we find there is physical, material connection among all bodies and atoms and no separation at all. You are already the whole of humanity, and connected to Earth, Stars, the Universe, whatever you call God. *Separation is an invention of the human brain.* When you see that, there is no more separation, no more yearning. You and whatever you understand as God are one already.

Other animals don't pull out their fur and feathers over this. Humans struggle with this because we are self-conscious. Other animals are conscious, but not self-conscious. When a cat feels hungry, she eats. It's finished. She doesn't sit around processing questions like "what about food in my future?" or comparing what she's eating with what the cat down the block is eating. A cat is already connected. Her thoughts don't interfere with her nap in the sun. She doesn't search for connection.

We don't have to search either. We're already connected. It's all that yearning, searching, and self-centered confusion over non-existent separation based on the human belief system in 'my own unique and separate self'—all that self-importance—that creates all the confusion, the loneliness, the psychological fear and suffering.

Shutting thought up allows the natural flow of connection and relationship. Not shutting it up artificially by holding your breath in some awkward position or muttering self-hypnotic words. Just by understanding what we've been discussing in this book—your self, your own evolutionary brain systems, what feelings and thoughts are and where they came from.

Then you can decide the right place for thought and the right place for insight into those thoughts and belief systems in order to put them aside so you can see what is really going on and what to do about it. Insight, the insight you need to really live your life well, requires the brain tissue to function, but it is not itself a material process and therefore does not reflect the personal or historical contents of the consciousness.

Just as people came to the Buddha, to Jesus, to Mohammed, to Lao Tzu, to Lord Krishna, so ministers, presidents, scientists, professors, ordinary people and students came to hear Krishnamurti teach the understanding of the human mind, the way it works, its psychological relationships to itself, to others, to life, work, to the world, time, space, the universe. When asked

**THOUGHTS WILL ALWAYS
COME UP. DON'T THINK ABOUT
THEM, WATCH THEM, LET THEM
PASS. DON'T FOLLOW THEM.**

by physicist David Bohm during their talks, as recorded in the book *The Ending of Time*, whether we could have a relationship with the Other or the Ground, as Krishnamurti referred to it, the great religious philosopher answered: "The Ground has certain demands: which are, there must be absolute silence, absolute emptiness, which means no sense of egotism in any form...Look, complete eradication of the self." And anyway, Krishnamurti said, "There is no 'me' at all, except the passport name and form; otherwise nothing. And therefore there is everything, and therefore all is energy."

You are already the whole of humanity, and not separate from but connected to Earth, Stars, the Universe, whatever you call God. Separation, the separation of particles into separate objects, as we have seen, is an illusion based on the way the human brain and our senses perceive things, not on actual boundaries. When you get that, there is no more separation, no loneliness. You and the Universe are one already.

EXPERIMENT: Talk with the Universe
from *Talk: Teen Art of Communication*

Silence is the language of the universe. Listening is the language of the universe. Looking, seeing, insight, understanding, these happen in the absence of words, thought, which are just the reflex of memory, the past. With the absence of the noisy chatter of the self-absorbed self, your atoms blend with all the atoms of the universe, instantly in communion.

All that talk which is the chattering of the self, its memories and knowledge and problems, all that it has been taught, must stop for us to touch the Infinite.

So, hush. It's the hardest thing for the jumping human brain, trained and used to occupying itself with problem-solving, to do. The begging prayers, the lists of needs or of sins, the mantras, the litanies, the comforting rituals of gurus, priests, shamans, rabbis, and mullahs may have their place in calming the brain. Yoga and breathing practices and so-called meditative practices may serve to still and oxygenate the body. But thought and its words must be silent for true meditation to take place.

Meditation means simply to pay attention, to be aware, of your thoughts and feelings. This is, after all, the way to know yourself, to understand yourself, to see what's going on with you.

EXPERIMENT

Don't Sleepwalk!

Pay attention—or get led around your life by everyone and everything!

❶ So, first sit down. Sit in a chair, or sit on the floor. Legs crossed or on the floor. Do not lean against the chair back or a wall. Back straight, shoulders down and relaxed. Lower your eyes to the floor or close them.

❷ Take a few deep breaths. Draw the air into your belly and bring it up through your diaphragm and into your lungs. Slowly. Let the breath out slowly, back down through your diaphragm. Tighten your belly and push all the air out. Keep your attention on your breath.

❸ Thoughts will occur. Watch them pass through your mind. Do not follow them. Note them, let them pass, bring your attention back to your breath. Watch your thoughts come and go. Do not hang on to any of them. Do not let them pull you away from where you are.

❹ The trick here is that there is no trick. Do nothing. There is nothing to do. When the mind quiets eventually, the *you* of you will not interfere with your connection to the universe and you will feel peaceful. In this stillness, your troubles and the troubles of the world fade away.

❺ After practicing meditation for a while, you will feel connections to everything and everyone. If you are lucky, you may hear the breath of the universe—and feel a high you have never known before.

Remember

Thoughts will always come up. Don't think about them, watch them, let them pass. Don't follow them. Don't lapse into scripts or daydreams. Eventually thoughts and scenarios, nervous lists of things done and to do, questions about what on earth you're doing just sitting there—all slow down. Leave spaces. It is in those spaces between thoughts, all that talk which is the chattering of the self, its memories and knowledge and problems, all that it has been taught, it is in those gaps that the Universe speaks to us. When the 'I' of us stops, we touch the Everything.

Truth Lies Beyond the Self

When Jesus said in the *Sermon on the Mount*, "The meek shall inherit the earth," when Buddha said in the *Dhammapada* [Teachings], "Life is suffering and the Self is the problem," when Lao Tzu said in *The Way of Life*, "If you never assume importance, you never lose it," they were all saying the same thing. This selfness we have all been educated to believe is so precious, is, in point of fact, not only a fluctuating, impermanent illusion, but the source of suffering and an impediment to seeing the truth. Truth lies beyond the self. Also, what the great minds of all cultures seem to be telling us is that nobody can hand you connection to everything and so the end of loneliness is up to you: it's a country you have to travel for yourself.

Note: We have all wondered, perhaps, why we keep trying for the moon, instead of traveling this country, the inner life of the mind and its connection to all Mind. It's because it is hard country to travel. Few people travel here, as there is no material benefit, no promotion, no security. But for those who make the journey, the beauty and joy and the end of loneliness is worth the difficulty. Freedom is the reward, from the suffocation and pain of the life of the little self. This land has a grand sweep, but no certainty. Those who go there have no choice.

It must be repeated that everyone, every brain, has the capacity to travel here. It is not only the genius, not only scientists or philosophers or the religious leaders—people like Galileo and Einstein, Christ, the Buddha, Krishnamurti, who can access whatever capacities lead to dialogue with the Universe. What they all agree on, though, is that thought and education and science alone are not the paths. David Bohm, the particle physicist, added that since we only use about 15 percent of our brain cells that we know about, imagine what all those unconditioned cells could do.

What it takes, they all say, is to be able to listen, and you can only listen in silence.

We need to be alone sometimes.

We need to sit and find silence.

Do It, and You Can

"Capacity comes with application," said Krishnamurti. "Do it, and you can."

"Just sit down, shut up, and stop whatever you're doing," said one of my mentors a long time ago when I was in a panic attack over the business of sitting still.

In my book *Stop the Pain: Teen Mediations,* I've gone into the many ways of inviting silence: sitting meditation; walking and other moving meditation from the marital arts to surfing, walking, dancing; breathing and relaxation practices; singing, chanting, prayer. All these are ways to quiet the brain's noise,

JUST SIT DOWN,
SHUT UP, AND
STOP WHATEVER
YOU'RE DOING.

so you can hear, watch, understand the ways of your self and your brain in daily life, and lose the psychological problems to live a life free of conflict, pain, depression, addiction, and loneliness. In this freedom, the Universe, the Light, will come to you uninvited, unbegged-for, uncajoled.

Talk to the Universe, to God, the Goddess, Whatever You Name the Nameless

Five minutes, to begin with, will do.

Simply sit. On the floor or under a tree, legs crossed, in a chair, not leaning back. Go where you can be absolutely quiet, undisturbed. Close your eyes, or if this leads to daydreams, drowsiness, flooding thoughts, lower your lids halfway and let light in. Unlike when you're having a talk with yourself, don't follow your thoughts and feelings to discover the underlying problem. Let go of whatever comes up and watch your breathing. Simply follow the breath. The usual lists and thoughts will arise, don't follow them, follow your breath. Mind your back, keep it straight to free your lungs to breathe properly.

Watch your emotions come and go, your reactions to thoughts, pain, pleasure. You will see nothing is permanent, none of these feelings lasts. Hatred, passion, greed, and their physical sensations pass without reaction. Just observe—as in, there's anger, there's anxiety, there's pleasure, there's boredom.

This silent focus on the breath is a marvelous opportunity to examine the inner country of one's own mind and its contents, its passion, its opinions, likes, dislikes, prejudices, pleasures, its urgencies.

You can bring your life's questions into this silence, like dropping pennies in a fountain. No insistence, no ritual prayers, just questions. Sometimes, the Universe answers, sometimes not. Sometimes the antenna, the satellite dish we can all turn toward the Universe, picks up the signal of the Universal Intelligence some people call God.

Sometimes not. The Universe comes uninvited, a blessing, not on demand. The more times you sit, the better your chances. You can't hear sound waves unless you know how to plug in.

Putting Your House in Order

At first, when you sit, all the mental horrors in your brain, all the things you are afraid of, all the arguments and resentments you've got going, all your nightmares and rages against what is unfair in your life, all your anxieties and problems will surface. Unless you sit still in a state of attention, a lot of your disorders may not become apparent. It is difficult to talk to the universe if your brain keeps raging at one of your parents or defending yourself against a teacher or figuring out ways to catch the mate of your dreams or thinking about what to wear to the Homecoming Dance. Before you can communicate with Eternity, you may have to address your arguments with people past and present, catch up on your schoolwork, clean your room, decide on what to wear, write a letter to your Adored of the Day (don't mail it), and generally put your mental house in order. Otherwise, your silence can turn into a screaming match or groveling for favors as if God were Santa Claus.

The spiritual teacher James Fowler reminds us in his book *The Present Moment: Meditations on the Practice of Contemplation*

THE UNIVERSE COMES UNINVITED,
A BLESSING, NOT ON DEMAND.

that providing we don't confuse religious institutions with the sacred, they may support, point, symbolize, but "it is important that we remain alive to the fact that the sacred is universal… expressed in different forms owing to cultural differences…

"If we lose sight of the fact that these differences are due to the impossibility of expressing the universal adequately, we are likely to assume that our own cultural forms are fundamental, and thus become vulnerable to the tragic division between religions, and even to the fanaticism of fundamentalism."

Organized religions are often used by unscrupulous people. Catholics have burned alive Protestants, Protestants murdered six million Jews, Jews are currently fighting Muslims, Mullahs are yelling for *jihad*, Holy War, and Hindus and Sikhs slaughter each other. Never confuse organizations with the sacred.

Religion can provide inspiration, but it is, as Fowler points out, a double-edged sword.

Drugs, Sex and Transcendence

There are those who swear that LSD and other mind-altering drugs are the best way to go beyond the self-centered fears of our brains and reach a state of transformation. There are those who swear by the self-forgetful ecstasy of sex, which is why women and men, in all the varieties and combinations, young and old, rich and poor, in all lands and cultures indulge in it so frequently.

Sadly, after a moment's or an hour's or even a week's escape, there you are again, back with nothing changed, no new insight into new behaviors that rewire your brain and make life happier for you.

Another problem, as Fowler points out, is that people who use drugs to alter their consciousnesses and experience a temporary exaltation often ascribe this experience to a superiority in themselves and set themselves up as gurus. They forget that moments of exaltation are gifts of the universe, and not to due to their own efforts. And always with us are the lazy or the immature in search of surrogate caretakers. They, and we, also forget that transcendental perceptions, moments of exaltation, moments of truth, cannot be transferred from one person to another. Each of us has to travel up that mountain of truth alone.

Sitting in Silence Is Not a Ritual

Churches and temples and mosques, circles of stone, all are places to contemplate and adore the Universe. By whatever name you give it. If candles and prayer beads and rituals, incense, statues and sun-pierced stained glass help to quiet the brain and point to the Eternal, why not. It is only when people mistake all these human constructions for the sacred itself that we lose communion with it.

All humans have a longing for the ultimate connection, to overcome their separateness from each other and the universe. We can escape or create substitutes for our longing not to be alone and lost in the stars. But ultimately, the longing to unite, to be part of all there is, never goes away.

But the Ultimate Reality, the Intelligence that is behind and infuses all this, is the Ultimate Reality of us all. You can ignore it, if you want, and stay unconnected, but your Intelligence is not created by the limited capacity of human thought based on neuronal circuits. Intelligence comes to you from insight, which does not have its source in the limited human brain.

Touching God

If only touching eternity had an easy technique! If only talking, imploring for help, or at least company from the gods, any of them, brought us an end to loneliness and the problems of having heads that contain the complex atavisms, the ancestral throwback genes in combination with modern technology that make us suffer, kill each other in our misery.

But there is no technique. There are the ways to begin to empty out our thoughts so the other can come in; that's all. And it's important to relate those lightning moments of connection to the business of everyday living so that too much mental disorder doesn't short-circuit your connection. Be kind. Do no harm, to yourself any more than to others. You are not always important, but the joy you carry is: it is the creative energy you carry that can help soften the world's pain.

Just remember we are all Earth's teenagers, half child, half adult. When silence becomes impossible, when the universal connection is full of static as it sometimes is, we have to talk with each other.

Learn to communicate with one another. Using words is what humans do.

Chapter Ten

SELF-DISCOVERY THROUGH TALKING AND LISTENING

■ ■ ■

"My generation of adults would have you function as cloned drones, soldiering, and breeding, voting, consuming, and thinking like the masses of people whose identity has been handed to them from the past...

"I challenge you to think for yourself, to be new all the time. Talk to each other. You will discover that talking also requires listening; to yourself, to others, to parents, teachers, bosses, sisters, brothers, friends, people you don't like, and to the universe.

"It is in listening that you learn to understand yourself and your conditioning. And it is understanding that sets you free of the past and its chains."

—R.E. Mark Lee, Executive Director,
Krishnamurti Foundation of America,
Oak Grove School Graduation Speech

■ ■ ■

Tools for Change

People are always going on about understanding yourself and changing, but they don't always give you hints or tools to use to go about this.

The self may be a trick played on us by our brains to give us a sense of security and continuity, but it's a powerful trick. After all, it's the brain's job to keep the body alive, and the way to do this is to make you feel self-important. As we have discovered, this makes us violent and defensive, even murderous. So, in the end, the self-importance we thought was a survival tool handed down from one generation to another is really an explosive device. It is guaranteed, with our present arms arsenal, to wipe humans out altogether.

It is not too late to realize this and stop. It is not too late to understand, through talking to one another, that we all share similar selves. Some of us can dance or sing or play better basketball, but emotionally and psychologically, we are pretty much the same, species specific, that is.

So we had better to learn to function as the community we are, instead of the separate selves we are *not*. We live alone inside separate bodies, but the whole human race shares the same consciousness. The whole human race thinks and feels pretty much the same way whether we do it in Swahili or Chinese, street talk or Harvard University vowels.

Best Tools to Understand Your Self

Humans have been thinking about this for thousands of years. They have discovered that the two best ways to understand yourself, and therefore everybody else, is through *dialogue—*

talking with each other—and *meditation*—listening to yourself talking to yourself.

The first, *dialogue*, is: Listen to yourself talk to other people.

The second, *meditation*, is: Listen to yourself talking to yourself.

Listen to Yourself when You Talk to Other People

Listen to yourself when you talk to other people, as well as listening to them. You will discover that your personal characteristics don't change much from person to person. You are passive or possessive, needy or giving, controlling or submissive, demanding or self-sacrificing, whatever you are with pretty much everybody. The sum of 'you' just works better with some people than others, and we call that a 'good' relationship.

I myself am continually shocked to discover that certain moods, thoughts, or feelings can seem to come out of nowhere: a sudden thrill, like a breeze on a hot summer afternoon; a plunge into dark despair, like a hole in the universe into which I have fallen; a quick onset of rage or joy that may take me places that don't make sense. Wes Niskar says, "Remembering my animal nature relieves my human nature." My brain-jerk reactions are evolutionary, and understanding this makes it easier to let go of them instead of giving them importance. And I have to learn over and over again that just because I have a feeling, a reaction, a thought, I don't have to do something about it. These knee-jerk reactions can just be let go, especially when they seem, incorrectly, to be caused from outside by other people, and are really caused from within.

TOOLS FOR CHANGE.

- Follow what is happening inside you when you are in a group of friends, what you feel, think, what you say out loud, what you keep to yourself.

- Be aware of what your brain is saying to you when you are with your family. Reactions to family are always the most extreme of all. And most of your belief systems come from family and their cultural conditioning, such as 'work hard, save your money, and you'll be happy', 'God will punish you if you disobey your parents.' These belief systems may be nonsense, but they have affected and infected your brain: watch out for them.

- Watch what you are thinking and feeling when this or that teacher is instructing or correcting you. Do you accept or reject this or that teaching, this or that teacher? Does any correction, criticism, or suggestion feel threatening to you? Make you feel worthless or shamed?

- Be aware of what goes on inside your head and body, your thoughts and feelings, when you are with a boyfriend, a girlfriend, your best friend—pleasure, jealousy, possessiveness, the adrenalin of excitement, a sense of security that also leaves you nervous lest it change or end.

Other People Are Really Good Mirrors of You

You will learn to understand yourself extraordinarily well when you listen to your responses, both inner and verbal, as you talk to other people. Conversation, dialogue, all interactions with others are extraordinary teachers about the nature of *you*. And, always, the more you understand about your self, the better you can make informed decisions about your behavior. Don't keep taking yourself by surprise!

Listen to Yourself When You Are Alone

- Don't just think your thoughts. Listen to yourself think, listen to the thoughts you are thinking. Be aware of your inner desires and fears, your criticisms of yourself and other people, your angers, your prejudices, your guilts.

- Ask yourself why you feel and think the way you do. See what is species evolutionary (According to most scientists, we separated from the other apes more or less 4 million years ago, and Homo sapiens has been around for about 200,000 years—so that we have had a pretty long time to collect fearful myths and misinformation as well as facts). See also what is personally evolutionary, your own parental, familial, cultural conditioning, as in 'think this', 'feel that', 'do this, not that.'

Pay Attention to Yourself and Ask Yourself Questions

If you are angry at someone at school or at work, are you really afraid? That she is more popular than you, therefore has the power to edge you out of the group, leaving you alone and unprotected? That he is stronger, better at games, more likely to take away possible mates, jobs, position, money?

① These are evolutionary and therefore understandable feelings. Without the pack a few thousand years ago, outsiders were not given food or protection and therefore died. Without mates and strength and tribal position, males were useless and ostracized.

Have an insight here, when such evolutionary feelings come up in you. These days there are nearly 7 billion people on earth, and in our country, plenty of food. You are not going to die because one person or one group doesn't like you. After all, there are plenty of people you don't like either, and your dislike doesn't kill them.

② Is the angry fear you hold for another person also based on your family or personal conditioning that to be popular with everyone makes you special? In some families, the popular child is more loved. In some families, the smart child is more loved. In some families, the prettier, handsomer child is more loved, or the most virtuous and best-behaved.

Have an insight into your family and cultural values. Realize that your attitudes about these values are simply automatic reactions, and have nothing to do with your actual value as a human being. This realization may change your evaluations of other people, may make you fear or envy them less often. Human beings face a perplexing problem: we all want to fit in (for protection) and we all want more importance (for protection). There's nothing to do about this primitive mental position—except to see it, and have a good, evolutionary laugh.

Whenever you are angry, or frightened, or upset with yourself, sit alone and be quiet for a few minutes, or a half an hour if you can, and pay attention to yourself and your thoughts and feelings. Determine their source and then decide on appropriate behavior. Know that the source of your feeling is *you*. Life happens. Other people happen. It's your reactions to everything and everyone that create *you*.

If you are upset about hurting someone else, it might be appropriate to discuss and make amends to them, if for no other reason so that you can stop talking to yourself about it. If someone has hurt you, it might be appropriate for you to discuss it, for the same reason. Get people out of your head, so you have some peace and quiet in there.

In any case, listen to yourself, your thoughts and feelings, and clear out your mental house every day, or your brain will drive you crazy.

One name for all this listening to yourself and what is going on in your own brain so you can quiet the noise in there, is meditation. Meditation is attention. Insight into problems can only happen in deep attention.

The point of all this attention and awareness is to understand your self and the way you work, your customary reactions.

Only by understanding, and by paying attention, can you be in charge of your own life and not, as we have said, be dragged down blind alleys by the wild, uncontrolled forces of your evolutionary feelings and desires and memories.

The self is all these memories, feelings, thoughts. Thoughts and feelings create the 'I', the 'me', the 'ego', and keep it alive. Most of our flaws and faults are neurobiologically evolutionary (genes) or else they are cultural ideas (memes). They are not personal. But we are still responsible for what we do with this inheritance of ancient instincts and contemporary conditioning. It is our responsibility not to repeat the harm they do or the prison they create or the inevitable suffering they can cause. Old commands, voices, reactions may not disappear from your brain. But they do not have to be obeyed or acted upon.

And the whole bundle must silence itself for what is really true to emerge, or we only see what *we* and our reactions are, not what is actually happening outside of us *out there*. *To find the truth of anything, the mind must be free of the self.*

This is the way of scientific investigation.

This is the way of meditation.

BIBLIOGRAPHY & YOUNG ADULT READING LIST

Many of the scientists whose work is fundamental to understanding what we know—and what we do not yet know—about how the brain works are mentioned in the text. So are many of the philosophers and metaphysical teachers.

The works listed here are accessible to anyone, with or without science or philosophy background. While some are not written specifically for young adults, they are written for the general audience and very readable, often humorous, and, rather than lecture, provoke thinking on the part of readers. This is particularly true of Stephen Jay Gould, Steven Pinker, and Stephen W. Hawking. I quote also from the 20th century philosopher J. Krishnamurti, as he has influenced some of our greatest science minds in areas of neuroscience and psychology.

Major sources for facts and statistics in this book, aside from the following texts, were newspapers, journals, magazines, especially *Time, Scientific American, National Geographic,* government publications, almanacs, public television specials, documentaries, and news broadcasts.

Many of the books listed have already been mentioned in the text of this book.

Teen Series Published by Bick Publishing House

Carlson, Dale and Hannah Carlson, M. Ed., C.R.C. *Addiction: The Brain Disease*, Madison, Ct. Bick Publishing House, 2010. Teen, young adult guide to the disease of addiction to substances, behaviors, oneself.

Carlson, Dale and Hannah Carlson, M.Ed., C.R.C. *Where's Your Head? Psychology for Teenagers.* 2nd edition. Madison, CT: Bick Publishing House, 1998. A general introduction for adults and young adults to

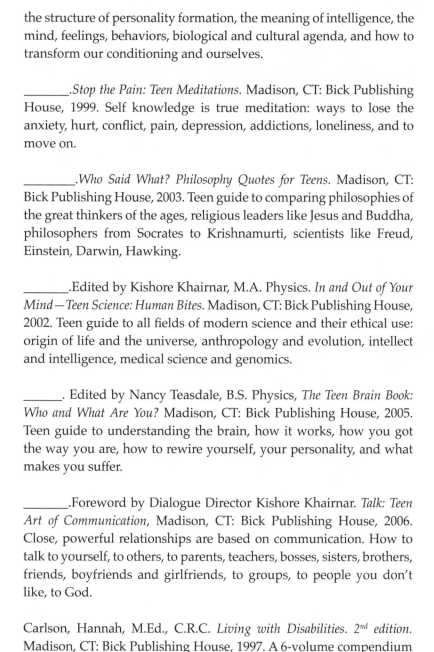

the structure of personality formation, the meaning of intelligence, the mind, feelings, behaviors, biological and cultural agenda, and how to transform our conditioning and ourselves.

_____.*Stop the Pain: Teen Meditations*. Madison, CT: Bick Publishing House, 1999. Self knowledge is true meditation: ways to lose the anxiety, hurt, conflict, pain, depression, addictions, loneliness, and to move on.

_____.*Who Said What? Philosophy Quotes for Teens*. Madison, CT: Bick Publishing House, 2003. Teen guide to comparing philosophies of the great thinkers of the ages, religious leaders like Jesus and Buddha, philosophers from Socrates to Krishnamurti, scientists like Freud, Einstein, Darwin, Hawking.

_____.Edited by Kishore Khairnar, M.A. Physics. *In and Out of Your Mind—Teen Science: Human Bites*. Madison, CT: Bick Publishing House, 2002. Teen guide to all fields of modern science and their ethical use: origin of life and the universe, anthropology and evolution, intellect and intelligence, medical science and genomics.

_____. Edited by Nancy Teasdale, B.S. Physics, *The Teen Brain Book: Who and What Are You?* Madison, CT: Bick Publishing House, 2005. Teen guide to understanding the brain, how it works, how you got the way you are, how to rewire yourself, your personality, and what makes you suffer.

_____.Foreword by Dialogue Director Kishore Khairnar. *Talk: Teen Art of Communication*, Madison, CT: Bick Publishing House, 2006. Close, powerful relationships are based on communication. How to talk to yourself, to others, to parents, teachers, bosses, sisters, brothers, friends, boyfriends and girlfriends, to groups, to people you don't like, to God.

Carlson, Hannah, M.Ed., C.R.C. *Living with Disabilities. 2ⁿᵈ edition*. Madison, CT: Bick Publishing House, 1997. A 6-volume compendium with sections that describe symptoms, origins, treatments for mental disorders, learning, disabilities, brain defects and injuries. Includes: *I Have a Friend with Mental Illness*. Also, *The Courage to Lead: Start Your Own Support Group, Mental Illnesses and Addictions*. Madison, CT: Bick Publishing House, 2001.

Additional Reading

Dennett, Daniel C. *Consciousness Explained*. Boston: Little, Brown and Co., 1991. Full-scale exploration of human consciousness, informed by the fields of neuroscience, psychology, and artificial intelligence, this is a funny, clear understanding of the human mind-brain. Not easy reading, but worth it.

Gould, Stephen Jay, Ph.D. *The Mismeasure of Man*. New York: W.W. Norton, 1996. Evolutionary biologist Gould's challenge to the hereditary I.Q. as a measure of intelligence and destiny.

_____. *Full House*. New York: Three Rivers Press, 1996. Humans are a twig on the bush of life, not the star on top of the tree. A funny, funny man, scientist, writer.

Grandin, Temple, Ph.D. *Animals in Translation*. New York: Simon & Schuster, 2005. The senses, brains, emotions, behaviors, talents we share with other animals.

Hawking, Stephen W., Ph.D. *A Brief history of Time: From the Big Bang to Black Holes*. New York: Bantam Books, 1988. A brief, popular, nonmathematical introduction, in words not equations, to astrophysics, the nature and origin of time and the universe. Hawking shows us how our 'world picture' evolved from Aristotle through Galileo and Newton to Einstein and Bohm (relativity and quantum physics—how we affect what we observe).

Johnson, Steven. *Mind Wide Open: Your Brain and the Neuroscience of Everyday Life*. New York: Scribner, 2004. Science writer undergoes MRI tests to better understand the neurochemistry behind love, sex, writing, tears, smiles, the brains own drugs, ideas. Fun to read.

J. Krishnamurti. *Education and the Significance of Life*. New York: HarperCollins, 1953. This influential philosopher founded schools in the United States, England, India, and here discusses the purpose of education, the difference between intelligence and intellect, brain and mind, the awakening of a new mind that continues to learn and inquire with both the scientific and religious/philosophy attitudes so that knowledge and our brains will not destroy us.

_____. *What Are You Doing with Your Life? Books on Living for Teens*. Ojai, California: Krishnamurti Foundation of America, 2001. Understanding how the human brain and mind, intellect and intelligence work so that your brain's self-knowledge will guide your life and actions, not the past with all its mistakes, and not outside authority either to be responsible for you or for your problems.

_____.Edited by R. E. Mark Lee. *The Book of Life: Daily Meditations with Krishnamurti*. HarperSanFrancisco, 1995.

LeDoux, Joseph, Ph.D. *Synaptic Self: How Our Brains Become Who We Are*. New York: Viking, 2002. The chemical and electrical connections between brain cells provide the biological base for memory, which makes possible the sense of continuity that creates the 'self.' The brain is physical, thought is physical, thought invents the self which is therefore physical, not some 'ghost in the machine' or some little mini-me in the head. Not an easy book to read, but well worth the time and trouble.

Nettle, John.

Panksepp, Jaak, M.D. *Affective Neuroscience: The Foundations of Human and Animal Emotions*. New York: Oxford University Press, 2005. The brain operating systems that organize the basic emotions of all mammals including us: fear, sex, rage, play, social bonding and care systems, and, in the human mammal, what happens to these basic systems when they connect with the human cortical thought system. On Panksepp's work are based many of the books on this list that deal with brain science. Not easy reading, but fundamental source material.

Pinker, Steven, Ph.D. *How the Mind Works.* New York: W.W. Norton, 1997. A long but witty, clear, and accessible read by a world expert in cognitive science. Pinker explains what the mind is, how the brain works, how it evolved, how it sees, thinks, feels, enjoys the arts, and ponders the mysteries of life. This is an extraordinary picture of human mental life, with insights that range from evolutionary biology to social psychology.

Restak, Richard, M.D. *The Secret Life of the Brain.* Washington, D.C., co-publishers, The Dana press and Joseph Henry Press, 2001. Companion to the PBS television series, this lavishly illustrated book explores the ages and stages of the human brain's development from infancy to old age and includes mental disorders and learning disabilities.

Ratey, John J., M.D. *A User's Guide to the Brain.* New York: Random House, 2002. 'Perception, Attention, and the Four Theaters of the Brain' is the book's subtitle. Perception captures incoming stimuli; attention, consciousness, and cognition process these perceptions; the major brain functions of movement, memory, language, emotion, and social ability work with this information; the result is behavior and identity.

Wells, Spencer. *The Journey of Man: A Genetic Odyssey.* Princeton, NJ: Princeton University Press, 2002. Human evolution and the spread of human beings 60,000 years ago from Africa south to Australia, north to the Steppes, and then 40,000 years ago West to Europe and East to Asia.

Further Reading

For further reading on how the mind and brain work, the psychology of human beings and their behavior, you might read what the great philosophers have written in earlier centuries. Their observation was no less acute without technology because of their capacity for objective understanding. The teachings of the Vedas, Krishna, Buddha, Lao Tzu, Confucius, Moses, Jesus, Mohammed, and, in this century, Mother Teresa, the Dalai Lama, and Krishnamurti are astute, and, by today's neuroscientific methods, quite accurate. A good source for teens in comparative philosophy is:

Carlson, Dale. *Who Said What? Philosophy Quotes for Teens.* Madison, CT: Bick Publishing House, 2003. The first comparative philosophy book targeted to young adult teens, it includes a thumb-indexed, easily referenced, readable introduction to the philosophies of the world. Teens can learn the great world philosophies and form their own.

WEB SITE RESOURCES

Links for Brain Science, Meditation, Philosophy, and Psychology

Type in: Self-Understanding, Neurobiology, Neuroscience, Evolutionary Psychology for Teens in a search engine. You will find excellent sites, but remember, sites change.

Understand Yourself and Others
www.2knowmyself.com/

Brain: the World Inside Your Head
www.pfizer.com/brain/

ThinkQuest
www.thinkquest.org

Explore the Brain and Spinal Cord
faculty.washington.edu/chudler/introb.html

The Journey of Man
www.NationalGeographic.com

The Secret Life of the Brain
www.pbs.org/wnet/brain/

INDEX

BICK PUBLISHING HOUSE
PRESENTS
Books for Teenagers

NEW!

**Understand Your
SELF**
by Dale Carlson and Kishore Khairnar, Physicist
Pictures by Carol Nicklaus

A PRACTICAL MANUAL FOR THE
UNDERSTANDING OF ONESELF
Self-Knowledge Is the Basis for Relationship
and the End of Human Loneliness

- Learn to understand your self on your own—not according to someone else's authority and rules
- Learn how the source of suffering is your own self in its fears and desires, AND HOW TO END THE LONELINESS AND PAIN
- Self-knowledge, self-understanding techniques, self-inventories
- Learn that you share an evolutionary, biological and species history with all human beings, as well as your own family, cultural and personal heredity
- Some of your heritage is good to enjoy—food, sex, sunlight
- Some of your inheritance you may want to change, stop acting on, before we all self-destruct as well as go on suffering—violence, greed.

YOUR HERITAGE NEED NOT RULE YOU

Dale Carlson: Author of dozens of books for young adults, with 3 ALA Notable Book Awards, the Christopher Award, YALSA Best Picks, VOYA Honor Book, 2 New York Public Library Best Books for Teens, 2 Independent Press Medals, 4 *ForeWord* Best Books of the Year

Publishers Weekly: "A practical focus on psychological survival."
School Library Journal: "Heady stuff...thought-provoking guide."
New York Times Book Reviews: Writes with intelligence, spunk, and wit."

Illustrations, Index, Resources, Websites
192 pages, $14.95, ISBN: 978-1-884158-36-0

BICK PUBLISHING HOUSE
PRESENTS
Books for Teenagers

ADDICTION
The Brain Disease
by Dale Carlson and Hannah Carlson, M.Ed., LPC
Pictures by Carol Nicklaus

- What is addiction?
- Addiction to substances
- Addiction to behaviors
- Addiction to the Self
- Treatment and Recovery
- Glossary of Addictions and Meanings

Young adult guide to the physical, emotional, social, psychological disease of addiction. What is addiction? Addiction to substances, behaviors, addictions to ourselves are explored. Self-tests, personal stories, treatment, recovery. Dictionary of addictions.

> "Breaks down the stigma regarding the nature of addiction. The raw truth regarding the physical, social, emotional, and psychological aspects of addiction, as well as help and recovery, are presented medically and through personal stories. This book unlocks the door of hope to any suffering from the disease of addiction to substances and/or behaviors. Carlson covers every base from medical neuroscientific information to self-tests to solutions in recovery."

> — Jason DeFrancesco, Yale-New Haven Medic

Illustrations, Index, Resources, Self-Screening Tests,
Help Telephone Numbers, Websites
114 pages, $14.95, ISBN978-1-884158-35-3

BICK PUBLISHING HOUSE
PRESENTS
A Young Adult Graphic Novel

COSMIC CALENDAR:
From the Big Bang to Your Consciousness
by Dale Carlson, edited by Kishore Khairnar, Physicist
Illustrations by Nathalie Lewis

Graphic Teen Guide to modern science relates science to teenager's world.

Our minds, our bodies, our world, our universe—where they came from, how they work, and how desperately we need to understand them to make our own decisions about our own lives.

- Teen guide to modern science
- Physics (no equations except for E-mc2)
- Natural history, physical laws of the universe and our Earth
- Evolution and origin of life, DNA and genomics
- Brain and body, intelligence—human, artificial, cosmic
- Dictionary of science terms
- Websites and links for all sciences
- Teacher's Guide and questions

Cosmic Calendar: Big Bang to Your Consciousness is the Graphic Edition of the award-winning *In and Out of Your Mind: Teen Science, Human Bites*, a New York Public Library Best Books for Teens.

"Contemplating the connectivity of the universe, atoms, physics, and other scientific wonders…heady stuff. Carlson delves into the mysteries of Earth, and outer and inner space in an approachable way."

— *School Library Journal*

"Challenges her readers with questions to make them think about the environment, humankind's place in the world, and how ordinary people can help change things for the better."

— *Voice of Youth Advocates*

Graphic Edition of NY Public Library
Best Books for Teens In and Out of
Your Mind: Teen Science
Illustrations, Index, 160 pages, $14.95,
ISBN: 978-1-884158-34-6

BICK PUBLISHING HOUSE
PRESENTS
Books for Teenagers

ARE YOU HUMAN, OR WHAT?
Evolutionary Psychology for Teens

We have evolved from reptile to mammal to human. Can we mutate, evolve into humane?

- Evolution has equipped us, not for happiness, but for survival and reproduction of the species.

- To survive, we are programmed for fear and pain: every one of us had ancestors who managed to survive, mate, and pass on the best adapted programs for staying alive.

- Our brain programs, hardware and software, have already conquered every other species: we've won, we can stop fighting.

- It's time to pay attention to our psychological welfare as well as our technology.

"*Are You Human, or What?* reminds us that we—as nervous, curious people—are not alone. Everyone suffers—and everyone can do something about it."

— *Meghan Ownbey, Teen Editor*

"This book challenges teen/young adult readers to examine their own culturally constructed views while emphasizing that compassion for all, not just 'me and mine' is the only way for each of us to survive."

— *January Welks, Teen Editor*

ForeWord Book of the Year
Illustrations, 224 pages, $14.95, ISBN: 978-1-884158-33-9

BICK PUBLISHING HOUSE
PRESENTS
Books for Teenagers

TALK: *Teen Art of Communication*
By Dale Carlson
Foreword by Kishore Khairnar, Dialogue Director

Close, powerful relationships are based on communication: Humans are wired for talk…communication must be learned. Teen guide to dialogue and communication. How to talk to yourself, to others, to parents, teachers, bosses, to sisters and brothers, to your best friend, to groups, to people you don't like, to the universe.

"Essential reading." — Jim Cox, *Midwest Book Review*

ForeWord Book of the Year
Illustrations, 192 pages, $14.95, ISBN: 1-884158-32-3

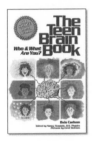

THE TEEN BRAIN BOOK *Who & What Are You?*
by Dale Carlson. Pictures by Carol Nicklaus.
Edited by Nancy Teasdale, B.S. Physics

Understand your own brain, how it works, how you got the way you are, how to rewire yourself, your personality, what makes you suffer

"Quality read for young adults." — *Midwest Book Review*

ForeWord Bronze Book of the Year
Illustrations, Index, 256 pages, $14.95. ISBN: 1-884158-29-3

BICK PUBLISHING HOUSE
PRESENTS
Fiction for Young Adults

THE MOUNTAIN OF TRUTH
Young Adult Science Fiction
by Dale Carlson
Illustrated by Carol Nicklaus

Teenagers sent to an international summer camp form a secret order to learn disciplines of mind and body so teens can change the world.

"Drugs and sex, both heterosexual and homosexual, are realistically treated...incorporates Eastern philosophy and parapsychology."
— *School Library Journal*

ALA Notable Book
ALA Best Books for Young Adults
224 pages, $14.95, ISBN: 1-884158-30-7

THE HUMAN APES
Young Adult Science Fiction
by Dale Carlson
Illustrated by Carol Nicklaus

Teenagers on an African expedition to study gorillas meet a hidden group of human apes and are invited to give up being human and join their society.

"A stimulating and entertaining story."
— *Publishers Weekly*

ALA Notable Book
Junior Literary Guild Selection
224 pages, $14.95, ISBN: 1-884158-31-5

BICK PUBLISHING HOUSE
PRESENTS
Books for Teenagers
Science & Philosophy

WHO SAID WHAT?
Philosophy Quotes for Teens
by Dale Carlson. Pictures by Carol Nicklaus

Teen guide to comparing philosophies of the great thinkers of the ages: form your own philosophy.

"Thought-provoking guide." —School Library Journal

VOYA Honor Book
YALSA Quickpicks for Teens
Illustrations, Index, 256 pages, $14.95.
ISBN: 1-884158-28-5

IN AND OUT OF YOUR MIND
Teen Science: Human Bites
By Dale Carlson.
Edited by Kishore Khairnar, M.S. Physics

Teens learn about our minds, our bodies, our Earth, the Universe, the new science—in order to make their own decisions. This book makes science fun and attainable.

"Heady stuff." — School Library Journal

New York Public Library Best Book for Teens
International Book of the Month
Illustrations, Index, 256 Pages, $14.95
ISBN: 1-884158-27-7

BICK PUBLISHING HOUSE
PRESENTS

Books for Teenagers
Psychology & Meditation
by Dale Carlson • Hannah Carlson, M.Ed., CRC
NEW EDITIONS

STOP THE PAIN: Teen Meditations
Teens have their own ability for physical and
mental meditation to end psychological pain.

- What Is meditation: many ways
- When, where, with whom to meditate
- National directory of resources, centers

"Much good advice...." — *School Library Journal*

New York Public Library Best Book for Teens
Independent Publishers Award
Illustrations, Index, 224 pages, $14.95; ISBN: 1-884158-23-4

WHERE'S YOUR HEAD? Psychology for Teenagers

- Behaviors, feelings, personality formation
- Parents, peers, drugs, sex, violence, discrimination, addictions, depression
- Joys of relationship, friends, skills
- Insight, meditation, therapy

"A practical focus on psychological survival skills."
— *Publishers Weekly*

New York Public Library Books
YA Christopher Award Book
Illustrations, Index, 320 pages, $14.95;
ISBN: 1-884158-19-6

**GIRLS ARE EQUAL TOO: The Teenage
Girl's How-to-Survive Book**
The female in our society: how to change.

- Girls growing up, in school, with boys
- Sex and relationships
- What to do about men, work, marriage, our culture: the fight for survival.

"Clearly documented approach to cultural sexism."
— *School Library Journal*

ALA Notable Book
Illustrations, Index, 256 pages, $14.95; ISBN: 1-884158-18-8

BICK PUBLISHING HOUSE
PRESENTS
Books on Living for Teens

TEEN RELATIONSHIPS
To Oneself, To Others, To the World
By J. Krishnamurti. Edited by Dale Carlson

- What is relationship?
- To your friends, family, teachers
- In love, sex, marriage
- To work, money, government, society, nature
- Culture, country, the world, God, the universe

J. Krishnamurti spoke to young people all over the world and founded schools in California, England and India. "When one is young." he said, "one must be revolutionary, not merely in revolt...to be psychologically revolutionary means non-acceptance of any pattern."

Illustrations, Index, 288 Pages, $14.95. ISBN: 1-888004-25-8

WHAT ARE YOU DOING WITH YOUR LIFE?
Books on Living for Teenagers
By J. Krishnamurti. Edited by Dale Carlson

Teens learn to understand the self, the purpose of life, work, education, relationships.

The Dalai Lama calls Krishnamurti "one of the greatest thinkers of the age." Time magazine named Krishnamurti, along with Mother Teresa, "one of the five saints of the 20th century."

Translated into five languages.
Illustrations, Index, 288 Pages, $14.95. ISBN: 1-888004-24-X

BICK PUBLISHING HOUSE
PRESENTS
Books for Health & Recovery

THE COURAGE TO LEAD—Start Your Own Support Group: Mental Illnesses & Addictions
By Hannah Carlson, M.Ed., C.R.C.

Diagnoses, Treatments, Causes of Mental Disorders, Screening tests, Life Stories, Bibliography, National and Local Resources.

"Invaluable supplement to therapy."
— *Midwest Book Review*

Illustrations, Index, 192 pages, $14.95;
ISBN: 1-884158-25-0

CONFESSIONS OF A BRAIN-IMPAIRED WRITER
A Memoir by Dale Carlson

"Dale Carlson captures with ferocity the dilemmas experienced by people who have learning disabilities...she exposes the most intimate details of her life....Her gift with words demonstrates how people with social disabilities compensate for struggles with relationships."

— Dr. Kathleen C. Laundy, Psy.D., M.S.W.,
   Yale School of Medicine

224 pages, $14.95, ISBN: 1-884158-24-2

STOP THE PAIN: Adult Meditations
By Dale Carlson

Discover meditation: you are your own best teacher. How to use meditation to end psychological suffering, depression, anger, past and present hurts, anxiety, loneliness, the daily problems with sex and marriage, relationships, work and money.

"Carlson has drawn together the diverse elements of the mind, the psyche, and the spirit of science...Carlson demystifies meditation using the mirrors of insight and science to reflect what is illusive and beyond words." —
R.E. Mark Lee, Director, Krishnamurti Publications America

Illustrations, 288 pages, $14.95; ISBN: 1-884158-21-8

BICK PUBLISHING HOUSE
PRESENTS

Books on Living
with Disabilities

by Hannah Carlson, M.Ed., CRC • Dale Carlson
Endorsed by Doctors, Rehabilitation Centers, Therapists,
and Providers of Services for People with Disabilities

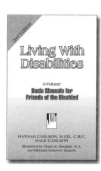

Living With Disabilities
6-Volume Compendium
ISBN: 1-884158-15-3, $59.70

INCLUDES:
I Have A Friend Who Is Blind
I Have A Friend Who Is Deaf
I Have A Friend With Learning Disabilities
I Have a Friend with Mental Illness
I Have A Friend With Mental Retardation
I Have A Friend In A Wheelchair

"Excellent, informative, accurate."
— Alan Ecker, M.D., Clinical
   Associate Professor at Yale

BICK PUBLISHING HOUSE
PRESENTS

Books on Wildlife Rehabilitation

by Dale Carlson and Irene Ruth
Step-by-Step Guides • Illustrated
Quick Reference for Wildlife Care
For parents, teachers, librarians who want
to learn and teach basic rehabilitation

Wildlife Care For Birds And Mammals
7-Volume Compendium
ISBN: 1-884158-16-1, $59.70

INCLUDES:
I Found A Baby Bird, What Do I Do?
I Found A Baby Duck, What Do I Do?
I Found A Baby Opossum, What Do I Do?
I Found A Baby Rabbit, What Do I Do?
I Found A Baby Raccoon, What Do I Do?
I Found A Baby Squirrel, What Do I Do?
First Aid For Wildlife

First Aid For Wildlife
ISBN: 1-884158-14-5, $9.95
Also available separately.

*Endorsed by Veterinarians, Wildlife Rehabilitation
Centers, and National Wildlife Magazines.*

ORDER FORM

307 NECK ROAD, MADISON, CT 06443
TEL. 203-245-0073 • FAX 203-245-5990
www.bickpubhouse.com

Name: _Carl Pattersons_

Address: _____

City: _Harlem NY_ State: _NY_ Zip: _60628_

Phone: _____ Fax: _____

QTY	BOOK TITLE	PRICE	TOTAL
	TEEN/YOUNG ADULT FICTION		
	The Human Apes	14.95	
	The Mountain of Truth	14.95	
	TEEN/YOUNG ADULT NONFICTION		
	New! Understand Your Self	14.95	
	Addiction: The Brain Disease	14.95	
	Are You Human or What?	14.95	
	Cosmic Calendar: From the Big Bang to Your Consciousness	14.95	
	Girls Are Equal Too: The Teenage Girl's How-To-Survive Book	14.95	
	In and Out of Your Mind: Teen Science: Human Bites	14.95	
	Relationships: To Oneself, To Others, To the World	14.95	
	Stop the Pain: Teen Meditations	14.95	
	Talk: Teen Art of Communication	14.95	
	The Teen Brain Book: Who and What Are You?	14.95	
	What Are You Doing with Your Life?	14.95	
	Where's Your Head?: Psychology for Teenagers	14.95	
	Who Said What? Philosophy Quotes for Teens	14.95	
	ADULT HEALTH, RECOVERY & MEDITATION		
	Confessions of a Brain-Impaired Writer	14.95	
	The Courage to Lead: Mental Illnesses & Addictions	14.95	
	Stop the Pain: Adult Meditations	14.95	
	BOOKS ON LIVING WITH DISABILITIES		
	Living with Disabilities	59.70	
	BOOKS ON WILDLIFE REHABILITATION		
	First Aid for Wildlife	9.95	
	Wildlife Care for Birds and Mammals	59.70	
	TOTAL		
	SHIPPING & HANDLING: $4.00 (1 Book), $6.00 (2), $8.00 (3-10)		
	AMOUNT ENCLOSED		

Send check or money order to Bick Publishing House. Include shipping and handling.
**Also Available at your local bookstore from: Amazon.com, AtlasBooks, Baker & Taylor
Book Company, Follett Library Resources, and Ingram Book Company.**

AUTHOR
Dale Carlson

Author of over 70 books, adult and juvenile, fiction and nonfiction, Carlson has received three ALA Notable Book Awards, the Christopher Award, the *ForeWord* Book of the Year Award, YALSA Nomination Quick Picks for Young Adults, New York Public Library Best Books for Teens, VOYA Honor Book.. She writes science, psychology, dialogue and meditation books for young adults, and general adult nonfiction. Among her titles are *The Mountain of Truth* (ALA Notable Book), *Girls Are Equal Too* (ALA Notable Book), *Where's Your Head?: Psychology for Teenagers* (Christopher Award, New York Public Library Best Books List), *Stop the Pain: Teen Meditations* (New York Public Library Best Books List), *In and Out of Your Mind: Teen Science* (International Book of the Month Club, New York Public Library Best Books List), *Talk: Teen Art of Communication, Wildlife Care for Birds and Mammals, Stop the Pain: Adult Meditations.* Carlson has lived and taught in the Far East: India, Indonesia, China, Japan. She teaches writing here and abroad during part of each year.

EDITOR
Kishore Khairnar, M.SC. Physics

Gold-medal physicist, professor of physics, mathematics, and computer science, Kishore Khairnar worked with the Electronic & Engineering Company in Mumbai, before creating his own NDT (Non-Destructive Testing) Company to provide engineering inspection services to industries all over India. He then joined the Krishnamurti Foundation India. He taught sixth to twelfth grade physics, electronics, and mathematics at the Rajghat Education Centre, organized dialogues and international gatherings for the study of the great philosopher Krishnamurti's teachings. As Chief Archivist at Rajghat in India and Brockwood in England, he worked at creating and computerizing the complete published works of Krishnamurti. He is publisher of the first Indian language translation of Krishnamurti's life, and of several English collections of the teachings in India.

Khairnar is coeditor with Dale Carlson of the American edition of *What Are You Doing With Your Life?*, the first Krishnamurti collection of teachings for teenagers. He is also the editor of Bick Publishing's *In and Out of Your Mind*, and *The Teen Brain Book*, and *Talk: Teen Art of Communication*. He and his wife, poet and music critic Professor Kalyani Inamder, live in Pune. He is Founder and Director of KET, the Krishnamurti Education Trust.

ILLUSTRATOR
Carol Nicklaus

Known as a character illustrator, her work has been featured in *The New York Times*, *Publishers Weekly*, *Good Housekeeping*, and *Mademoiselle*. To date she has done 150 books for Random House, Golden Press, Atheneum, Dutton, Scholastic, and more. She has won awards from ALA, the Christophers, and The American Institute of Graphic Arts.